SUCCESS SPEAKS FOR ITSELF...

Critical Praise for D. A. Benton and
Lions Don't Need to Roar...

▼

"Good impressions can take work....Benton's style is not to tell people what to do, but to help them figure out a better way."
—*Seattle Times*

▼

"In *Lions Don't Need to Roar*, Debra has identified some of the more subtle but critical success factors essential for a person to rise to the top in today's business world. Her chapters on the importance of listening, asking questions (vs. always having the answers) and 'Life at the Top' are particularly insightful."
—**John D. Bowlin, president, Oscar Mayer Foods Corporation**

▼

"Highly readable...for people with talent to match their ambitions."
—*Working Woman*

▼

"If you've got the right stuff for a business career, Debra Benton can tell you how to make the powers-that-be take notice. Her books give you the people skills to achieve your goals."
—**Bob Berkowitz, author of**
What Men Won't Tell You But Women Need to Know,
host of CNBC, "Real Personal"

▼

"Her work is aimed at giving people control over their destiny."
—*New York Times*

▼

more...

LIONS DON'T NEED TO ROAR

USING THE LEADERSHIP POWER OF PROFESSIONAL PRESENCE TO STAND OUT, FIT IN AND MOVE AHEAD

D. A. Benton

WARNER BOOKS

A Time Warner Company

Copyright © 1992 by Debra Benton
All rights reserved.

Warner Books, Inc., 1271 Avenue of the Americas, New York, NY 10020

Visit our Web site at http://warnerbooks.com

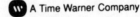 A Time Warner Company

Printed in the United States of America
First trade printing: August 1993
10 9 8

Library of Congress Cataloging-in-Publication Data

Benton, Debra.
    Lions don't need to roar : using the power of professional presence to stand out, fit in, and move ahead / Debra Benton.
        p.   cm.
    ISBN 0-446-39499-8
    1. Office politics.   2. Business etiquette.   3. Success in business.   I. Title.
HF5386.5.B46   1992
650.1—dc20   91-51179
                                                              CIP

Book design by Giorgetta Bell McRee
Cover design by Diane Luger
Cover photo by Tim O'hara

First, I would like to thank my family, especially my parents, Teresa and Fred Benton, for helping me maintain a sense of humor throughout this project.

Second, I am most appreciative of Pat Straley, who provided constant constructive critique and who really made the computer work in producing several "final" versions.

Third, my editor at Warner Books, Fredda Isaacson, and my agent, Michael Cohn, who along with Susan Meltsner gave the book its "professional presence."

Finally, needless to say, I am indebted to several people who provided encouragement, support, and recommendations: Lee and Mary Alexander, Curt Carter, Frank Childs, Sherry Gerity, J. M. Jones, Dr. Kelly Kesler, Nancy Albertini, Arthur Oldham, Ray Storck, Hugh Sullivan, Inge Trump, Dennis Wu, and especially . . . Rodney Sweeney.

—Debra Benton,
Benton Management Resources
Fort Collins, Colorado

CONTENTS

PART TWO
FIT IN—THE ART OF RELATING

PART THREE
MOVE AHEAD—THE ART OF SELF-REALIZATION

LIONS DON'T NEED TO ROAR

1

The Basis for
Business Success—Be Yourself

• Roger's career was at a standstill. He had been passed over for a half dozen promotions in the last two years.

"I don't understand it," he said. "I come into the office early and stay late. I make all my deadlines, even if I have to work nights and weekends to do it. You'll never catch me huddled in the hallways shooting the breeze with my colleagues or see me grandstanding at staff meetings. I'm paid to do a job and I do it. I do it well. I'm smarter and more productive than half the guys who started at the same time I did. So why are they heading departments and up for vice-presidencies while I'm stuck in limbo, doing the same things at the same level I've been at for the past few years?"

• Mark, an ambitious young editor, found himself in a similar situation. However, he had begun to figure out why he wasn't zooming up the corporate ladder as planned. "I know my stuff," he said. "I'm good at what I do. But I'm a washout at office politics. Every time I turn around I'm either saying something I shouldn't or kicking myself for keeping my mouth shut when I should have spoken up. Making small talk with authors and

1

agents at cocktail parties isn't my strong suit either. I break into a cold sweat just thinking about it, and even when I tell myself, 'Get out there and make a good impression. Go up to that guy and introduce yourself. He won't bite your head off,' I can't bring myself to do it. I just freeze up in social situations—and it shows. My boss has mentioned it more than once. She keeps telling me to loosen up, that I'll never get ahead in business unless I learn to make the right impression and get along with people in *any* situation."

• Karen, a bright, capable, lifelong overachiever, received a similar message from her boss—right before he fired her. "You work hard," he explained. "You're honest and smart and competent, but you're aloof and seem determined to do everything all by yourself. We work as a team here, and you're not a team player. You don't relate well to people. You have no people skills."

Karen was shocked. Devastated. And, once her boss's words sank in, she was confused. "Why hadn't hard work or productivity—and not something as intangible as 'relating to people'—been the deciding factor?" she wanted to know. She couldn't believe that "people skills" really mattered that much.

• The head of a large architectural firm knew that they did. He had this to say about an employee whose job was in jeopardy, despite his wonderfully innovative ideas and award-winning designs: "Jerry's probably the most talented architect working here, but he has no tact. No finesse. No feel for the human side of the business. His abrasive 'I know what I know and everyone else doesn't' attitude has cost us one lucrative contract already, and we can't afford another fiasco like that. If he can't learn to deal with his colleagues and clients more appropriately, we'll have to let him go."

As a consultant and lecturer hired by small businesses and huge corporations worldwide, I have advised, observed, and trained thousands of people like Roger, Mark, Karen, and Jerry—hard-working, smart, honest men and women who were getting nowhere, getting into trouble, and even getting fired because they: "had poor chemistry," "couldn't develop rapport," "had no impact," "were sharp but didn't step up to the plate and take control of the power that could be theirs," "lacked people skills."

If you are capable, efficient, dedicated, and diligent but not advancing in your chosen field or as rapidly as you had hoped, chances are that you have become bogged down for those same reasons. Even if hard work, long hours, and technical expertise are enabling you to hold your own right now, unless you are proficient in the human side of business as well, you could be in for a rude awakening in the future. As Roger, Mark, Karen, Jerry, and countless others have done, at some point in your career, you will find out that *competence alone does not lead to professional success.*

To get to the top, stay there, and be truly successful in the business world, you need: *presence* as well as performance; *emotional strength and the ability to get along with many different types of people* as well as skill and intellect; and *courage, luck, and the ability to communicate effectively* as well as hard work.

This book is about those attitudes and abilities. It shows you how to develop them and how to use them to make your professional life as satisfying and successful as it possibly can be. It also leads you along the path others have taken on their way to the top.

LEARN FROM THE BEST

Like most of my clients, I was raised on the Protestant work ethic. I heard the usual adages about little strokes felling great oaks and early birds catching the worm, and I had no qualms about putting my "shoulder to the wheel and nose to the grindstone" or trying again if at first I didn't succeed. By putting those principles into practice, I racked up a list of accomplishments before entering the business world and sincerely believed that as long as I continued to work hard, I would continue to achieve my goals. But instead of my being as successful in business as I had been at other endeavors, I found my potentially brilliant career grinding to a halt just two years after it began.

Like Karen, I got fired because I didn't relate well to people—and I too was stunned. Before that fateful day, no one had even mentioned the importance of people skills to me. No course I had ever taken included the human side of business on its syllabus. That lack of knowledge cost me my job. I was bound and determined not to let it happen again.

After going through outplacement and discovering a great deal about the real world, job hunting, career planning, and myself, I persuaded my outplacement counselor to teach me the business; and then "hung out a shingle" for myself as Benton Management Resources. I began sharing with other people who had lost their jobs the insights that I'd gained after losing mine. I also started interviewing successful businesspeople—nearly two thousand of them over a ten-year period. I looked for patterns in their experiences that would help me teach other success-seekers how to think, act, and relate.

By using what I learned in my own life, I gained a reputation in the world of business. My work expanded to include lectures and training seminars as well as private consultations with executives, politicians, and media personalities who wanted to enhance their personal presence (or as they put it in Europe, have more "charisma"). I also was able to extend my "research" into the higher echelons. I sought out the best—the men and women who had climbed up the slippery ladder of success in their field and now sat on the top rung.

I interviewed and studied more than a hundred chiefs—chief executive officers (CEOs), chief operations officers (COOs), and the big chiefs (company presidents). As you will see from the quotes that appear throughout this book and the list of acknowledgments, I spoke with leaders in the media, professional sports, government, nonprofit organizations, manufacturing, cable TV, advertising, finance, and other fields. I observed these top people in formal business situations: at board meetings, in the midst of international negotiations, before and after speeches, during media interviews and in executive offices. I also spent time with them in informal settings: on boats, in private jets, on golf courses, at sporting events, and at office Christmas parties. In some instances, I even met and spoke with their secretaries, children, spouses, ex-spouses, and other "right-hand people" to gain their perspective of Mr./Ms. Big.

I listened, watched, remembered, and learned that *top people are not magical, blessed or dramatically different from you or me*. They simply have skills and outlooks that the rest of us may not have—but can get. We all have the capacity to make it to the top of our fields and stay there. What we often lack are the tools and techniques to convert our potential into productivity, effectiveness, and success. Over the years, I have taught thousands of people what those tools and techniques are and how to use them. I have written this book to teach those same things to you.

TOP PEOPLE

"Are forward thinkers, strategic planners and motivators who guide and encourage people toward optimum performance."

—THOMAS NEFF
President, Spencer Stuart

"Create a path for themselves in their company, one that stretches four to five years into the future. They have stature. They aren't afraid to make decisions. They got to the top by being flexible, unflappable, rolling with the punches, understanding change, reacting quickly to change, being willing to make mistakes and communicating both as a giver and a listener."

—JOHN CALLEN, JR.
Chairman, and CEO, Ward Howell International

"Can function with many styles and in many environments. They have the ability and sensibility to listen. But the number-one factor that sets them apart from the pack is an aura of energy and actual energy. All high-powered executives have that."

—BILL MORIN
Chairman, Drake, Beam, Morin Inc.

SUCCESSFUL PEOPLE HAVE ENERGY

1. *Physical energy* to meet the physical requirements of the job. With it, they give 100 percent to the task at hand, persevere, demonstrate loyalty, and show the enthusiasm that puts them first in line for promotions.
2. *Intellectual energy*, which enables them to understand every nuance of a job and become proficient at it. Intellectual energy makes it possible to perform brilliantly some of the time and competently the rest.
3. *Emotional energy*, which they use to understand themselves as well as understand and interact with others. With it, they control the effect they have on people; know just how to connect with and relate to various individuals in various situations; and make a positive impression, no matter where they are or what they're doing.

While all three levels of energy are required for career success, emotional energy is by far the most important, and it can be developed, cultivated, and fine-tuned. The purpose of this book is to show you how to do that—because *emotional energy and the people skills that go with it are what will get you to the top and keep you there.*

PEOPLE SKILLS ENTAIL CERTAIN QUALITIES

Subtlety

When Admiral Elmo R. Zumwalt, Jr., retired chief of operations, United States Navy, assumed command of a ship that had the voice radio call name SAPWORTH, he immediately changed it to HELLCATS and saw morale improve even before the name change went into effect.

Appreciation

When I accompanied John "J" Madden, president and CEO of John Madden Company, into the health club he owned, I watched him greet a maintenance man, chef, front desk manager, and three members by name and saw all of their faces light up in response to the recognition they'd received.

Profitability

While a teenager working as a valet, Bill Daniels, chairman of Daniels Communications, doubled his tips when he said "Yes, sir (or ma'am)," to his customers rather than just "Yes."

Style

"Two people can spot the same issue. Two people can say exactly the same thing about it. But the one who presents his idea in the proper style can help you solve the situation while someone who uses the improper style won't solve it (or even get to finish saying how he *would* solve it)."

—JEFF SMULYAN
Owner, the Seattle Mariners

People skills can be learned and practiced until they become second nature to you. When you have emotional energy and people skills, you can:

• *Stand out* to get in—by making favorable first impressions and having a positive impact on the people around you.

> "One strong suit will help you a lot. You need at least one outstanding quality—originality, intelligence, common sense, vision or energy—plus people skills."
> —**ROBERT BARTLEY**
> *Editor*, The Wall Street Journal

• *Fit in* to get promoted—by looking as though you belong at the top and getting along with many different kinds of people.

> "The one who makes it to the top has luck, works hard, is bright and believes in team work. Although it's not a personality game, you have to be personable, likable, and able to get along."
> —**J. RICHARD MUNRO**
> *Cochairman and co-CEO, Time Warner Inc.*

• *Stand out and fit in* at the same time—by doing what others don't without going to extremes.

> "I have a twenty-two-year-old son who started his first job six weeks ago. He currently believes it's only substance that counts, that getting his work done is all that's necessary. I try to tell him how much talent goes unnoticed, that he needs to attract the attention of those above him. That holds true for anyone who wants to advance. You need to do the job properly but also display an eagerness to do more. Look alert when you're bored; if you finished the job, do your damnedest to look interested. Instead of looking like a bumbler or a slouch, look like a bright-eyed kid ready to go. Be

aware of your physical presence and conduct yourself just a tad in excess of what is required."

—GORDON PARKER
Chairman, president, and CEO,
Newmont Mining Corporation

Standing out to get in

plus

Fitting in to get promoted

plus

Standing out *and* fitting in (by doing what others don't without going to extremes)

adds up to

Business success.

CAN YOU MAKE THAT EQUATION WORK FOR YOU—AND STILL BE YOURSELF?

Absolutely!

"Developing into yourself is a lifelong process, but while you are going through it, you can take on behaviors that fit you. Through active observation and active listening . . . I adopted a style that *became* me."

—WILLIAM WALLACE
President and CEO, Home Life Insurance Company

To get to the top and stay there, you may have to change the way you typically think, act, and relate to other people in certain situations. But you do NOT have to become someone you're not. In fact, *to be successful you have to be yourself.* You simply have to "be yourself" more consciously, purposefully, and positively than you may have been in the past. That means:

- being aware of what you are thinking, saying, or doing at any given moment;
- consciously choosing attitudes, words, and actions that work to your benefit and avoiding those that work against you;
- adopting new behavior patterns that are consistent with who you are now and, more important, with who you *want* to become.

THE BOTTOM LINE

If the person you want to be is someone who is easily trusted, memorable, impressive, credible, genuine, likable, and effective from the first encounter on, then you are reading the right book. The chiefs I interviewed learned how to set themselves apart from the rest, and you can too. From this book, you'll learn to control your actions so you can control your effect, so you can control your career and have more power and more impact, and make more money!

I

STAND OUT—
THE ART OF MAKING
AN IMPACT

2

Make and Maintain a Favorable First Impression

If you control your actions, you can control your effect to control your career. That statement applies to every facet of doing business, but its impact is most apparent and extremely important during your initial encounters with people. When you are meeting someone for the first time as well as during the first moments of any interaction, the first impression you make is crucial. Top people know that:

> "I don't get a lot of time with anyone. In the space of five or ten minutes, I must convey interest, enthusiasm, and energy."
>
> **—ANDREW SHERWOOD**
> *Senior partner, The Goodrich & Sherwood Company*

> "I want to have the most impact possible as quickly as possible."
>
> **—ALEX MANDL**
> *Chairman and CEO, Sea Land Service, Inc.*

Successful people make *effective* first impressions. They stand out and fit in at the same time in order to be trusted, respected, and intriguing. "This isn't going to be an ordinary encounter," is the message chiefs convey, and they convey it in a matter of seconds. Although they are not always striving to be *liked*, they do want to be *remembered* favorably.

FAVORABLE FIRST IMPRESSIONS DON'T "COME NATURALLY"

• A female lawyer delivering a speech to an association meeting I attended stood at the lectern for twenty minutes reading from a script that she held in place with her left hand—and kept her right hand inside her blouse collar clutching her bra strap.

• I had been told that the man I'd be meeting for lunch was "an absolute genius at marketing." He did indeed prove to be brilliant—and enthusiastic. Each time a brainstorm hit him, he excitedly shared it, gesturing broadly—with soup spoon in hand—and splattering his tie, the tablecloth, and me with Manhattan clam chowder.

• "I have the hardest time getting my male colleagues to take me seriously," a woman who attended one of my seminars complained. As she stood in front of me and elaborated, she shifted her weight from one foot to the other so that her body—and her ample breasts—swayed back and forth. With her bright silk blouse also catching my eye, it was practically impossible not to notice this motion, and I suspected that it was at least partially responsible for her difficulties.

The people I just described were memorable, all right. But did they really want to be remembered for clutching a bra strap, splattering soup, or swaying their breasts? Of course not. What they conveyed about themselves was not what they had hoped to convey, and the impression they made was not favorable to them—*because they were not in control of their actions.* In fact, they weren't even aware of them—or of their effect.

When you act without awareness, you: miss opportunities to make a positive impact; all too often make a negative one; unwittingly sabotage yourself and your chances for success.

UNFAVORABLE FIRST IMPRESSIONS DON'T "GO AWAY" EASILY

> "The perception you have of people from the first usually proves to be true."
>
> —DAVE LINIGER
> *CEO, RE/MAX International*

Whether you agree or disagree with Liniger's opinion, the fact is that people draw conclusions about you from the moment you make your first entrance and *they seldom change their minds*. They size you up in an instant, and whether they decide to "write you off" or conclude that you are "okay" and worth getting to know better, they rarely question their snap judgments. It may not be fair (or what you want to hear), but if there is a choice between two comparably qualified people, the one who makes a better first impression will be chosen.

> "Most people don't have time actually to figure you out. So their initial perception of you is very important. If you make a bad impression, you have to get over the bad impression. If it's good, you can go on to step two."
>
> —HAROLD ELLIS
> *Chairman of the board, CEO,*
> *Grubb & Ellis Company*

People form their impressions of you by looking at the outside and making assumptions about what's on the inside. They take you at face value. It's your responsibility to establish that value—and establish it quickly.

You have a limited time to show people "what you're made of." If you:

- anxiously rush into a room and hurry to your seat, scarcely acknowledging anyone or anything in your path;
- slink in like a scared puppy;
- slip in surreptitiously so that you can come *and* go without anyone noticing that you were there.

then you waste precious time.

If you are:

- distracted;
- rude;
- obviously unprepared;
- cold;
- inappropriately familiar;
- tripping over yourself to impress and flatter others;
- or about as responsive as a corpse.

then you are unwittingly establishing an impression that you will have to work hard to overcome. You may never get to erase it. At the very least you will have to grind your way out with competence.

The effort required to make a favorable first impression is less than the effort required to undo an unfavorable one. Even when someone you meet seems to be in too much of a hurry or seems too preoccupied to pay attention to you, your efforts to create a good first impression pay off.

NO MATTER WHAT YOU DO, CONTROL WHAT YOU ARE DOING

Although you can't actually control other people's feelings or their reactions to you, they base their perceptions on what they *see*—and you *can* control what you show them.

Generally speaking, you'll want to make a first impression that is *realistically favorable*—neither creating expectations you can't fulfill nor leading others to believe that you are less capable than you actually are. Being obvious and affected or relying on gimmicks (such as having oversized chairs for everyone but yourself so that they feel small in comparison to you or placing your desk on a raised platform so that you tower over anyone who enters your office) is usually inappropriate and ineffective.

There are no hard-and-fast rules governing the specific behaviors you should use to make an initial impact. The point is not to make a particular first impression or the same impression all the time, but to make the impression that fits your immediate circumstances and best suits your purpose. An initial impact that would be all wrong in one situation could be just right in another.

For instance, a defense lawyer meeting with a district attorney for the first time might deliberately decide to show up wearing an old suit with his collar unbuttoned, his shirt rumpled, and his hair unkempt. By leafing through files, hesitating before responding to questions, and generally demonstrating a laissez-faire, almost apathetic, attitude toward his client, he would create the image of himself as being a bumbler and not much of a threat to the DA. Under most circumstances, making such an impression would be unwise. However, if the defense lawyer then showed up in court impeccably dressed, immaculately groomed, and intellectually as sharp as a tack, his first impression would have been extremely effective. It would have disarmed the DA—as the defense lawyer undoubtedly intended it to.

Though you usually won't need to be as manipulative or as

deceptive as that defense lawyer when making *your* initial impact, you will want to:

- determine the impression you want to make in a particular situation;
- figure out what you need to do or avoid doing in order to make that impression;
- then follow through.

Controlling even small, seemingly insignificant actions can positively influence other people's perceptions and improve your chances for success.

Nine Ways to Make and Maintain Favorable Impressions

1. *Use your entire physical being to express yourself.* People believe what they see. They remember what they see. And you can control what they see—the angle of your head, your facial expression, your slumped or well-postured shoulders, the fit of your suit, the position of your legs, hands, arms, or feet and much more.

Your physical presence is the foundation on which you build your credibility. So, analyze and thoughtfully plan how you will present yourself physically. Pay attention to the nuances of your physical presence during the interaction. That way, if the encounter is unsuccessful, you will recognize actions that had a negative impact, know how they held you back, and be able to change them the next time around. You will also be able to recognize what you did well and remind yourself to repeat that behavior during future interactions.

Act in a slow, controlled, purposeful manner. Whether you scratch your head, adjust your eyeglasses, straighten your tie, or search for the scrap of paper with your budget estimates on it, do it with purpose. Almost anything you do will be okay, if it is done on purpose. If you make moves too rapidly, too abruptly, or without awareness, chances are that you will sabotage yourself by looking nervous, flustered, or "quirky."

2. *Have a physical game plan.* When Louis Mattis, chairman and CEO of Sterling Drug Inc., holds a "directive" meeting (one in which he is in command and doing the directing), he sits behind a desk in a big imposing chair facing whomever he's meeting. There's no doubt in anyone's mind about who's in charge during that sort of interaction.

"But only four of about one hundred meetings last year were conducted that way," Mattis explained. The others were what he called "conversation" meetings in which he and the other person mulled over mutual problems, brainstormed solutions, and freely exchanged ideas. Those meetings were conducted in the sitting area of his office with all parties in relaxed, comfortable, equal positions on a sofa or settee.

In each instance, Mattis *physically set the stage to accomplish a purpose he had decided upon ahead of time.* And that is what it means to have a physical game plan.

In advance, determine the effect you want to have on others and use the "props"—the right attitude, the right actions, the right setting, and even the right prearranged placement of people—that are most likely to create that effect.

Do whatever will help you achieve your objective during a particular interaction. Put yourself in a dominant position or others in more favorable positions—if that positioning fits the situation. Create an atmosphere that is conducive to your purpose—whether that purpose is to get people to listen to your ideas or to talk about theirs.

Chiefs seldom admit to coming up consciously with physical game plans—they just do the right thing from repeated experience. While *you* are gaining that experience, knowing what you are going to do and how you are going to do it will have a calming effect on you and help you feel more confident during various encounters. Even if things don't work out as planned (and they seldom do), having a game plan is still a better place to start than trying to make a favorable impression without one.

3. *SHOW people what you mean—with coordinated words and actions.* Television networks race to be the first on the scene so their viewers can see as well as hear the news. They know that people remember best what they receive visually. As much as 85 percent of the information absorbed during any conversation is transmitted nonverbally.

To get your message across and make a favorable impression, you must not only state but also demonstrate what you mean with *purposeful* movement and *appropriate* nonverbal communication.

You sabotage yourself when you say "What a great idea" in a flat, unenthused tone or when you nervously chew your lower lip and stare at your feet while swearing that you're looking forward to the challenge presented by a new project. Instead:

- Plan what you want to say.
- Think of ways to corroborate what you are saying, using gestures, facial expression, tone of voice, inflections, and so on.
- Then say *and* show what you mean, making sure to synchronize your verbal messages and your nonverbal signals.

4. *Don't respond to distractions.* Not long ago I met with a man who had attended one of my seminars and was determined not to respond to distractions. He was talking while leaning back in a desk chair that tilted back and had wheels. Then he placed his hands behind his neck, and the extra weight from that action combined with his body weight caused the chair slowly, but unavoidably, to tilt farther and farther back. But he didn't move. He continued his conversation, and when he and the chair finally fell to the floor, he said (without skipping a beat), "See, Debra, I listened to you."

Although it's not necessary to go to such lengths yourself, do your best to *ignore distractions.* Keep your eye on the ball. Don't let the furniture, the air-conditioning fan, the sirens outside, the airplane overhead, or the wart on an interviewer's nose break your concentration or prevent you from establishing and maintaining your physical presence. Stay on track. If you want to control your effect on others, you can't let inanimate objects control you.

5. *Develop by subtraction.* To make and maintain favorable impressions, you do not have to adopt dozens and dozens of new behaviors. Simply relax and stop shooting yourself in the foot. Retire your sabotaging actions—the *ineffective* things you say or do.

Become more aware of what you are doing and the effect you have on people. Observe their reactions. If you are getting the response you want, continue. If you aren't, change your actions.

6. *Do the opposite of what most people do.* Many of us are afraid to deviate from the norm because we mistakenly believe it will hinder us and reduce our chances for success. Yet, countless breakthroughs in business have begun when someone broke the rules.

Doing what others don't is, in fact, the key element of an effective executive presence. It is what this entire book is about. And it does *not* mean wearing a yellow business suit. Your goal is to stand out while still fitting in. You have to add distinctions that highlight your individualism and make you memorable—in moderation. Extremely eccentric behavior will single you out *unfavorably*.

Staying within the realm of acceptable business behavior, set yourself apart from the crowd. Observe what most people do, and, instead of doing the same thing, do something else. When reasonable and appropriate, do the opposite. If others:

- hurriedly rush into someone's office, you pause;
- select the chair closest to the door, you select the one farthest from it;
- sit around a boardroom table with their elbows on the table, hands clasped and shoulders hunched over, you sit back in your chair with relaxed, open arms;

- state claims and repeat platitudes, you ask probing questions;
- are in a group with people who sit when asking questions, you stand up to ask your question;
- act like stodgy stuffed shirts, you act human and humorous;
- stop initiating sales calls at the end of the day or during bad weather, you make them at that time.

As one financial investor put it, "the majority is usually wrong." So, rather than blindly following other people's lead, be just different enough within the boundaries of the situation to be remembered positively.

7. *Be flexible.* At the beginning of the business day, a former CEO who sold his company to a larger one and now acts as a consultant to the new owners asks himself, "Who am I today?" He needs to "know what costume to wear—what I want to accomplish and how I should act to accomplish that." He is not talking about role playing but flexibility—the ability to draw upon different aspects of his personality in different situations. If he's meeting the new CEO on the golf course, he might call upon the friendly adviser side of himself, making jokes and small talk in between suggestions given as a father might offer them to his son. If he's going to the same golf course with the head of a rival company, he might be more guarded and cagey as he tries to pump the other person for information without being pumped himself. In another setting he might be playful or stern or practically dictatorial.

Successful people know that no matter how effective a particular style might be, they cannot rely on that same style under all circumstances. They change their style to meet their objectives, to make the impact they want to make in a particular situation. They know that rigidity works for only a limited time in limited situations and that their actions will affect one person differently than they will affect another. Even someone they know well may be receptive to a certain approach one day and repelled by it the next. If they are going to deal effectively with people over a long career, they must be flexible.

Being flexible does not mean being wishy-washy and constantly changing your position on an issue. And flexibility is not an excuse to allow yourself wild mood swings. (That can create tremendous insecurity in the people around you.) Instead it is, as one executive put it, "being chameleonlike in a positive way"—being exuberant in one setting, restrained in another, sometimes relaxed and casual, sometimes serious and formal, *depending on the situation.*

Because you, like all human beings, are multifaceted—and *not* one-dimensional—you can be flexible without "faking" or "putting on an act." To have a positive impact, you don't have to change your personality. You can choose one or a combination of actions from the wide range of behaviors available to you—and still be yourself.

8. *Be willing merely to "go through the motions" for a while.* Much of what it takes to make a favorable impression (and to get to and stay at the top) seems stilted or contrived when you first see it on a printed page and feels odd or uncomfortable when you first try it for yourself. *Try it anyway.*

Old habits are comfortable. Because you are used to them, the same old things *feel* right—even when they're wrong. You *became used to* those actions by repeating them, and you can become used to new behaviors the same way. Take on a behavior that doesn't quite fit you yet and practice it until it does. If you go through the motions physically, your attitude and emotions eventually catch up. On the other hand, if you try to wait for a new technique to *feel* right before accepting its merit or putting it into practice, you'll wait forever.

9. *Follow the four-minute rule.* Although you have only seconds to make a favorable impression, *that is all you need.*

"In retail, they have what they call a 'twelve-second factor'—that's the time you need to capture a buyer's attention with your product, design, package, color, and positioning. The same time limit applies to making an impression as an individual."

—R. MICHAEL FRANZ
President and CEO, Murata Business Systems, Inc.

Another CEO told me, "You have approximately *three seconds* to establish your presence. Two seconds to size up the situation and how to approach it, then one second to correct yourself if you're wrong."

I happen to subscribe to the *four-minute rule* and advise my clients to be consciously aware of and conscientiously control their actions for at least the first four minutes of every encounter. Obviously, you'll want to maintain a positive presence throughout the interaction, but if you tune in extrasensitively and stay on top of your behavior for those first four minutes, you will almost always be able to have the effect you want to have.

Successful people are constantly aware of how they are being perceived—and adjust their actions to control their effect. Once you achieve an edge by making a favorable first impression, you have to hold on to it with moment-to-moment behaviors that reinforce your initial impact and have a lasting effect:

- make sure you are competent;
- develop, hone, and use plenty of people skills;
- continue to practice and improve the techniques I describe in this chapter and other key elements of an effective executive presence that I describe throughout this book.

3

Use Your Head to Express and Impress

On my way to the offices of Price Waterhouse, I noticed a man walking across the lobby toward me. Although I didn't know him (or have any reason to believe I ever would), I made eye contact with him. As he got closer I did not look down or away. Maintaining my relaxed, slightly smiling facial expression, I focused my full attention on him and, just before we passed each other, gave him one slow, deep, purposeful nod of acknowledgment.

That man turned out to be the person I had been scheduled to see at Price Waterhouse. He was responsible for hiring in-service trainers, and I easily secured a three-day consulting assignment.

Three years later, that client still remembers our encounter and the conclusion he drew from it: if I could make such a positive impact on him with a simple, subtle action, his people could learn to affect their clients the same way. He hired me because I had quite literally *used my head*.

Successful people get ahead by using their heads—intellectually and *physically*. They:

- have relaxed/ready facial expressions;
- smile;
- keep a level head;
- occasionally and purposefully nod, rather than incessantly bob, their heads;
- make and maintain eye contact as well as use their eyes to help them communicate effectively.

USING YOUR HEAD EFFECTIVELY

Look Relaxed and Ready

Take a moment to:

1. Relax your brow.
2. Relax your jaw.
3. Relax your feet.
4. Say the word *money* or *sex* (whichever you prefer) and then leave your mouth in that position with: your lips open (apart about one-eighth of an inch); the corners of your mouth turned up slightly; and a little roundness in your cheeks.

Your face is now in what I call the "relaxed/ready" position. Like the "ready" stance you take in a sport, such as golf, tennis, volleyball, or skiing, it is the position for beginning a peak performance. You look awake, alert, alive, open, confident—and prepared for anything that comes your way.

A relaxed/ready expression is a natural expression for the human face. It is the facial expression of any infant who isn't hungry, wet, or physically uncomfortable. Most toddlers wear it. But somewhere along the line, a good many of us have lost it. Perhaps, during our childhoods, we were told once too often, "wipe that stupid smile off your face," "close that trap," "you are only to speak when spoken to," "I don't want to hear those words out of your mouth again," or "only idiots smile without a reason."

In self-defense, we replaced our naturally open and receptive facial expressions with scowls, grimaces, or bland, blank, unemotional masks.

As adults, we may have mistakenly come to believe that we had to "look serious" if we wanted to:

- be taken seriously and treated professionally;
- avoid appearing overly accommodating or phony;
- hold our cards close to the chest and not give ourselves away;
- make sure we didn't wear our hearts on our sleeves, seem high-strung, or appear irrational by showing too much emotion;
- not be judged as too light-hearted, frivolous, lazy, or lethargic to do what it takes to advance in our careers.

As a result, we adopted zombielike, stone-faced, perpetually worried or borderline-angry expressions. We may call that expression "businesslike" and think that it comes with the suits we wear, but in reality, along with our smiles and openness, we've wiped the personality off our faces. We look like terrorists or as though we haven't eaten in days.

Some of us frown or scowl or wear a flat, expressionless face when we are thinking or listening intently and aren't paying attention to the effect our facial expression has on other people. One company president was frowning a few years back while walking down the hallway at corporate headquarters. Soon afterward the company's chief financial officer came into the president's office and asked, "What's the bad news? I heard in the hallway that the business is going to hell." Apparently an office worker who had observed the president's facial expression jumped to a conclusion, passed along her "findings," and started a panic. There were no financial problems. But people make assumptions based on what they *see*, and the president *looked* like a deeply troubled man.

In my opinion, the only people truly justified in having totally flat, expressionless faces are prison inmates. For their own protection, they resort to a facial position with no muscle or eye movement and maintain it by developing keen peripheral vision. They are on guard against attack and not open to communication.

The rest of us and especially those of us who hope to get to and stay at the top in our fields—*unless we are talking, chewing, or purposefully using our faces to convey our emotions—should maintain our relaxed/ready facial position.*

Get into the habit by practicing when you aren't on the hot seat. While jogging, lifting weights, listening to the minister, listening to your boss, listening to your spouse, making a telephone call, or engaging in any other routine activity during the course of a day, look relaxed and ready. You'll quickly discover that it's the look others like to see—and the one they are most likely to respond to favorably.

Smile More

Smiles draw positive attention to you and make you (and others) feel at ease.

> "The people attending [the leadership conference] were all self-employed salespeople who had earned enough to come to the annual convention, and they were somewhat suspicious of the new Japanese ownership. Then, the Japanese company president walked onstage, and in his imperfect English, but with heartfelt emotion, read a speech he'd written himself. He smiled. He smiled *a lot*.
>
> "After the speech, he spent five hours having his picture taken with two hundred prizewinners in the sales leaders' circle—and he smiled throughout. Those salespeople were so impressed with the guy and his friendly, approachable manner, that they were ready to carry him out on their shoulders like the star quarterback on a championship football team."
>
> —DAVID CHAMBERLAIN
> *Chairman, president, and CEO, Shaklee Corporation*

CONFIDENT, SUCCESSFUL PEOPLE SMILE

Top people smile more frequently than people on any other rung of the career ladder—and not just because they make more money.

> "Why do I smile? Because it reflects my mood and improves attitudes—mine and others."
>
> —JOHN BUTLER
> *President, Financial Programs, Inc.*

Smiles:

- convey self-acceptance and an accepting attitude toward others;
- inspire confidence in the person who is smiling and boost the confidence of the person who sees the smile;
- spread an attitude of good cheer, making people in the smiler's vicinity feel good about him, themselves, and their jobs.

By smiling, you can:

- intimidate and/or confuse an adversary;
- soften the blow when delivering bad news and say difficult things with the most beneficial outcome possible;
- reduce tension;
- keep your cards close to your chest (contrary to popular opinion, you do not give yourself away by smiling and can, in fact, conceal shock, confusion, fear, or information you are not yet ready to make public knowledge behind an amiable grin);
- build a reputation as a winner (especially if you smile whether you win *or* lose).

Smiling:

- is an instant energizer;
- makes you appear approachable, friendly, relaxed, open, and comfortable;
- shows others that you are good-natured, have a sense of humor, and enjoy life;
- improves your voice quality by relaxing your throat muscles;
- makes you look younger;
- takes fewer facial muscles than frowning;
- and more cheaply, quickly, and safely than a face-lift, produces similar results.

When shouldn't you smile? When you're being buried—and when you are firing or disciplining someone or when your expression would unintentionally contradict your words.

If you think that it doesn't look "macho" to smile, you're right. It doesn't. But machismo won't take you as far as smiling will. In fact, you probably don't need to be macho at all when your goal is to be effective. You *do* need to smile. I can still remember the midlevel executive sent to me for counseling by his boss, who told me, "He could be a great senior executive if only he smiled more." One glum man (who was not a chief) confided, "When I was a kid, people said I had a silly grin, so I got rid of it. I still smile on the inside, but no one knows it."

Smiling on the inside doesn't cut it. Neither does refusing to smile because you are self-conscious about your teeth, lips, or mouth in general. If you can't smile, you can't lead.

There are more than enough frowns in the business world today—and a huge deficit of smiles. In the circles in which you travel, the majority may be dead serious, pessimistic, and downtrodden. *Don't be like the majority.*

Whether you are an introvert or an extrovert, when you get to be Mr. or Ms. Big, you will need to smile. So start practicing right away.

KEEP A LEVEL HEAD

In our culture, we expect businesspeople to be "level-headed": to think clearly and rationally, and also physically to hold their heads high and face people head on. Someone who doesn't is perceived as: laying his head on his mother's chest for comfort; vulnerable; easy; overly attentive; begging; subservient; losing; stupid; tired.

A bowed head conveys insecurity, shyness, and defeat. You can see its effect when one person is attacking, criticizing, or otherwise "coming down" on someone else. Nine times out of ten, the person receiving the aggression bows his head. He looks like a victim, and the aggressor treats him as such. A bowed head is the body-language equivalent of having a sign on your back reading "kick me."

A person who tilts his head to the side fares no better. You won't see a president of the United States cocking his head to one side. A cocked head conveys confusion and simple-mindedness. (You can practically hear the "duh? . . . I don't get it.") You could also be perceived as being flirtatious, vulnerable, or seductive— which is why so many women photographed for "girlie" magazines are posed with their heads tilted to one side. It's unlikely to be the effect businesspeople want to have.

Whether bowed or cocked to one side, a tilted head will always make a less favorable impression than a level one.

When your head is level, you:

- look more controlled and sure of yourself;
- look like a winner;
- improve your posture;
- appear more energetic;
- improve your voice quality;
- are in a better position to "look 'em in the eye."

Simply holding your head level may seem trivial or insignificant. But it's the sort of subtle behavior that can make or break someone's confidence in you. Whether receiving good news or bad, keep a level head. It is the head position top people maintain.

Don't Bob Incessantly. Nod Purposefully.

I'm all for letting people know that you are listening to them. By actively listening—conveying your interest and understanding and encouraging speakers to say more—you make a favorable impression as well as learn more from the person who is speaking to you. There are a number of *effective* ways to do that. But bobbing your head like a toy dog with a spring neck placed on the rear window of a '57 Chevy is NOT one of them.

In the oil business, the arm of an oil rig that bobs up and down is called a dickie bird. People engaged in a friendly conversation sometimes end up looking like them—and it is not a positive, in-control, or useful way to look. Head bobbers invariably appear overly anxious or too eager to please. To avoid that fate and still show attentiveness and understanding, try:

- an occasional, slow, deep, purposeful nod (it's surprisingly difficult to do and will take some practice before you feel comfortable with it);
- verbal "nod" (with a level head and without bobbing, utter affirming sounds such as "mmhm," "uh-huh," or "ah ha");
- squinting or raising one or both eyebrows for a second or two, again with your head level.

MAKE EYE CONTACT AND USE "EYE" COMMUNICATION

Top people look others in the eye. Their direct gaze can send a very attentive, supportive "I'm listening to every word" message. Or it can resemble two leveled pistols boring in on a victim.

Or it can fall anywhere on the spectrum between those two extremes.

Eyes can make people feel *comfortable* . . .

> "Top people emote and connect with their facial expressions. You can see the twinkle, the energy in their eyes."
>
> —PETE CARPENTER
> *President, CSX Distribution Services*

. . . or *uncomfortable*. "When I'm dealing with difficult bureaucrats, I just look them in the eye and wiggle my eyebrows," says Bob Graves, founder of the National Marrow Donor Program, who has big, bushy eyebrows that make this technique especially effective.

Chiefs control *where* they look, and they don't avoid eye contact. The higher up the ladder someone goes, the longer he will maintain eye contact. When he encounters people of lesser rank, they invariably break eye contact before he does. I've walked down a hallway with many a Ms. or Mr. Big and watched one person after another avert his or her eyes. Clearly, if you want to stand out when *you* meet a chief (or anyone else you hope to impress), you can't nervously lower your gaze as other people do. Maintain eye contact.

Successful people seem to listen with their eyes as well as their ears. Explaining how his father, Art Linkletter, was able to interview children successfully for the popular television series "House Party," Jack Linkletter said, "Before he spoke to the child, Dad would totally lock into eye contact with that child. Sometimes that meant reaching up to a child's chin and gently turning his head toward him. But, by making that eye contact, he let the kids know, 'Hey, I'm talking to you and you're talking to me.'"

That approach works just as well with grown-ups. Effective eye contact and communication helps you:

- look more alert, attentive and alive;

- concentrate on what's being said to you;
- appear unafraid;
- convey to others that they are important and that you are listening to them;
- look confident.

Here are five options for communicating effectively with your eyes:

1. Look at someone's entire face, rather than only boring into his eyes.
2. Watch people's lips while they're speaking; "reading" lips helps you hear what they are saying.
3. Focus first on one of the speaker's eyes and then on the other eye. It can make you, as the listener, look particularly attentive.
4. Break some of the tension that often results from uninterrupted eye contact by purposefully averting your eyes to jot down a note or periodically looking over the other person's shoulder instead of right at him.
5. Practice maintaining eye contact until you can hold someone's gaze a second longer than formality requires. That extra second gives you an aura of confidence and says, "I can take the heat."

Whether you smile or keep a level head, use a relaxed/ready expression or effective eye communication; controlling small actions prepares you to take control and maintain it when you tackle big issues.

Once you get used to using your head and begin to see its positive effect, you'll wonder how you got along without this simple way to make a positive impression. But don't "beat yourself up" over the ineffective things you have done or the effective things you have failed to do in the past. It's okay to have been wrong. What's unforgivable is to stay wrong.

4

Making an Entrance—
The Pause That Impresses

When a successful person enters a room, you know it. He or she makes an entrance. Not a flamboyant, look-at-me-I'm-special type of entrance, but one that says, "I'm here. I'm ready. I know who I am and I know what I'm doing. No matter what happens, I can handle it."

TOP PEOPLE GET NOTICED—IMMEDIATELY

Watch chiefs and you'll see men and women who walk into a room and quickly take stock—sizing up the situation, noticing the people around them, and getting a sense of the general mood or what might be on people's minds. They move directly and deliberately toward the person to whom they wish to speak and frequently make a comment before they even shake hands.

With a combination of attitude and actions, top people emanate an aura of self-confidence and benign control when they make entrances. They are in control of themselves, the situation, and their effect on others.

Of course, most chiefs hold meetings in *their* offices or board-rooms and don't have to have others watch them make an entrance. Instead they enter the room first and watch everyone else come in. However, when they do have to walk into territory that is not their own, successful people are apt to enter and *pause*.

The president and CEO of a *Fortune* 500 company was scheduled to speak before a large gathering. After an impressive list of his accomplishments had been read, he was introduced. He stood up, climbed four steps onto the stage, walked the full length of the stage, stopped at the podium, adjusted his eyeglasses, removed his notes from his suit pocket, arranged them on the lectern, and looked at the audience. Then he looked back down at his notes and finally, more than two minutes after his name was announced, began to speak.

"Kill or be killed," he said when I asked him why he had deliberately delayed for so long. He had taken control of his audience by making an entrance that included a planned, purposeful pause.

A pause that impresses is *not* necessarily a long pause. In some instances, it lasts no more than a split second. It is *not* a pause of hesitation or indecisiveness—leaving you standing in a doorway looking lost or confused. But it *is* a purposeful, strategic, physical, or conversational "break in the action."

> "Yesterday, the vice-president for manufacturing came into my office to discuss a personnel issue, and I missed half of what he was saying because I was still thinking about the serious budget problem that came up in my previous meeting. That wouldn't have happened if he had caught my attention and switched my focus before bringing up his issue. Some sort of pause would have done that.
>
> "I pause to give people a chance to respond to my entrance and get on my wavelength. I just can't take it for granted that they're fully listening to me, and I can't assume that they're concentrating on the same thing

I'm concentrating on. So I pause and usually bring up a transitional topic, something diversional like the weekend football game or the weather or anything else that gets us on common ground."

—**PHIL WILKINSON**
Director, AT&T Network Services

A purposeful pause ensures that you don't go unnoticed. Nervous, self-conscious people hurry. Confident people pause. They know that every second of silence or minute of transitional conversation pays for itself with the added attention it brings to them or the point they hope to make.

When to Pause

1. *Pause when entering any room.* Don't sneak into or out of meetings, even if you are late or have to leave early. Try briefly stopping in the doorway to make your presence known without disrupting or upstaging someone who is speaking. Never assume an apologetic air, race in like a white tornado, or tiptoe in timidly.

2. *Pause when entering the limelight.* Even a slight pause allows you to get a little extra from being on center stage. And as the gentleman I described earlier did, you can use an extended pause to gain control of an audience.

"Take control of a room or leave," A Washington, D.C., lobbyist told me. "If you're not in control, get out. Make up a reason to leave if you have to, but get out." While it's easier and more necessary for people at the top to do it, if you don't take the time to capture your audience's attention at the outset, you may have to find ways to extricate yourself from "losing" situations as well.

3. *Pause during one-to-one interactions.* Strategic silences allow you to emphasize important ideas and maintain a strong presence throughout any encounter. They led to a complete turnaround in my relationship with one client.

This particular client had always been slow to pay for my services, and anticipating that he would be once again, I called as soon as I had completed the assignment and set a time to meet, present my report, and be paid.

He agreed.

I showed up at the appointed time and said, "I'd like to explain the report and get my check for five thousand dollars."

He replied, "Your check is in the mail."

I was not pleased but pleasantly and matter-of-factly responded, "We agreed I would be paid today. Perhaps you could issue a duplicate check. I'll be glad to return the one that comes in the mail."

My client's face turned red as he leapt to his feet and, practically shouting, said, "I don't need you to come in here bill collecting. I don't like your attitude, I don't even like the way you comb your hair, and you can get out of here!"

Shocked and dumbfounded, I left his office as ordered and went to the ladies' room to think about the situation. Twenty minutes later I asked my client's secretary to request another meeting with her boss.

Thirty minutes after that, he allowed me back into his office. He gestured for me to sit down but I did not. I paused in the doorway. I walked halfway into his office and paused again. Taking my time, I paced, purposely pausing between direction changes.

Finally, I stopped. I remained standing, placed my hands on the back of a chair, paused once more and then spoke. "I don't care about the money but I *do* care about my business reputation," I said and paused again. Looking him dead in the eyes and maintaining a relaxed facial expression, I continued. "I am not your secretary, servant, or your wife. You owe me an apology. I'm going to go through this report I committed to do. Then I'll leave." I paused. Sat down. Explained my report. Stood up. Paused. Walked toward the door. Paused, turned, and nodded good-bye.

Much to my surprise, that client, who had been so harsh and borderline abusive an hour earlier, stood up, started around his desk toward the door and giving me a signal to wait, asked, "May I shake your hand?"

Although I was taken aback, I said "yes," and as he shook my hand, he apologized. Then he handed me the check, which hadn't been mailed after all.

I turned to leave again but stopped, turned back to him, paused, and nodded good-bye one more time.

It was his turn to be surprised. With his voice conveying a combination of awe and amazement, he declared, "You're going to be *very* successful." Although that meeting took place several years ago, neither of us has forgotten it, and my client has done his part to make his prophecy come true. He continues to use my services—and pays for them promptly.

Clearly, a pause can have a powerful impact. It not only attracts positive attention to you and any message you want to convey, but also:

- nonverbally announces your presence;
- helps you look like a competent, confident contender;
- gives you time to take a deep breath and relax;
- is more courteous than rushing onto another person's turf;
- provides you with an opportunity to look people in the eye;
- gives you a chance to calmly size up any situation.

To get to and stay at the top, *take your time*. You can set yourself apart with only the slightest pause. Try it. People won't exclaim, "Look how he pauses," but they will think, "Hmm, something about that person is different from the rest. I'd better pay attention."

5

Get a Good Grip on the Situation—Shake Hands

While eating alone in a Los Angeles restaurant and observing people (as I frequently do), I noticed that the restaurant manager was interviewing people for a job. He went to the entrance, met each applicant, shook that person's hand, and walked him over to a corner table. They both sat down and a brief exchange took place. Then the candidate stood up and left. Each entire interaction took less than five minutes.

Before my meal was served, the manager had gone through that routine eight times. During my meal another nine people were greeted and conversed with in the same manner. By the time I paid my bill, I was very curious about the manager's interviewing technique and walked over to ask him what he learned about job applicants in such a short amount of time. "Whether or not I want to spend more time with them," he replied and went on to explain that he usually made his decision before he asked his first interview question. "I talk to everyone," he said, "but I actually make up my mind while I'm shaking their hands."

People draw conclusions about you in seconds (or at the most minutes) and you "start the clock" with your handshake. Your handshake makes an impression. It's up to you to control the impression it makes.

Top people shake hands as if their reputations and hundreds of thousands of dollars are riding on that handshake, which is often the case. But even when it isn't, their grip is anything but wimpy.

When he met me in his reception area, John Ziegler, Jr., president of the National Hockey League, extended his hand and shook mine. Grasping my hand firmly, he held it a split second longer than decorum demanded; and I felt the strength of his personality, as if it originated in his toes, flowed through his five foot eight frame and down his arm to my palm. He was memorable and impressive within seconds of our meeting.

Never underestimate the significance of a handshake. Politicians study and practice to make sure that their hand-to-hand contact with constituents conveys sincerity and strength. Heads of state stage greetings to create the "right" shake of power, and no meeting of international leaders begins until they have been photographed shaking hands. Handshakes were deemed so important by one major U.S. air carrier that in the first quarter of 1990 all first-class cabin flight attendants received a memo instructing them to "say a personal good-bye to each first-class passenger, use their name and *shake their hand*."

A "WINNING" HANDSHAKE

It helps convey certainty, confidence, and competence. It lets others know that you're someone who honors commitments and can be trusted to "do business on a handshake basis." As a manufacturing president who makes it a practice to shake hands regularly with each and every one of his managers put it, "If my people couldn't give me a competitive handshake, I'd be afraid to send them out into the world."

Also, a winning handshake is not a hurried flea-flicker get-it-out-of-the-way handshake. You won't look like a winner when you rush, or are too loaded down with briefcases, purses, books, and papers to extend your hand, or if you timidly wait for the other person to make the first move. To get a grip on any situation and make a favorable impression with your handshake, begin by:

- pausing to focus on the person you are greeting;
- smiling;
- looking that person in the eye.

Then initiate. Reach out. Extend *your* hand to anyone with whom you are doing business—male or female.

When two men meet, they usually shake hands immediately, but they tend to hesitate before shaking hands with a woman. Despite the words of wisdom they may have found in old etiquette books or heard from their mothers, my advice to men is: don't wait. When meeting in any business-related setting, you should shake a woman's hand just as readily as you would shake that of a man.

Neither should women hesitate to extend their hands to men—and women. I have found that businesswomen share their male counterparts' reluctance to greet women with a handshake, and I advise them to overcome their discomfort by extending their hands consistently to all women at all times and under all circumstances.

Guidelines for Giving a Good Handshake

1. Respect people's preference for space and distance. Generally speaking, someone from Wyoming or rural Texas requires more distance than someone from New York City or other urban areas.
2. Clasp palm to palm, not palm to finger. A palm-to-palm handshake is firm, controlled, and rarely described as wishy-washy, or "like holding on to a dead fish." Women, in particular, benefit from this technique. By tilting their open palm upward at a slight angle so that it meets a man's

palm, they avoid having their fingers pinched by men with powerful grips. When that happens and the woman winces in pain, both parties feel uncomfortable and their interaction gets off to a poor start.

3. Talk to the person whose hand you are shaking.
4. Hold on for a split second longer than duty requires.
5. Be firm but not so forceful that you cause discomfort. Assert pressure without getting into a power play. Try to match the other person's grip—not outdo him or her.
6. If you wish to convey additional warmth, use two hands, placing your free hand on the clasped hands or on the other person's arm or shoulder.
7. Briefly and purposefully pause again as you retrieve your hand.

Shaking Hands with Someone You're Meeting for the First Time

Volunteer your own name as well as listen for the other person's name—and remember it. Most of us hear people's names for the first time during a handshake. The trouble is that at that moment most of us are also a bit nervous and uncomfortable. Distracted by our own discomfort, we may not even hear the other person's name, or we immediately forget it. To help you remember people's names (and it is *very* important to do so):

- relax; memory improves when you are at ease;
- immediately repeat the name out loud, using it in the very next comment you make to that person;
- if possible and appropriate, use it again within a few minutes;
- at the first available opportunity, jot the name down somewhere.

Like all the other actions that help you make a positive impact on others, following the guidelines for shaking hands and remembering names may feel odd and uncomfortable at first. Keep trying. By doing it repeatedly, you will learn to do it well—and naturally.

6

Give the Right Touch—
And Not Too Much

Consider this scenario: A boss has gathered his key people together so that he can "pass the baton of power" to Joe, who will be running the business in his absence. Standing at the head of a long boardroom table with all eyes upon him, the boss begins, "As you know, I'm leaving for a six-month sabbatical. While I'm gone, Joe is going to be at the helm." The boss points toward Joe, who is seated to his left, and continues. "Look to Joe for help with any questions or problems. He'll be in charge."

Now, consider this alternative: In the same situation, the same boss makes the same announcement. Only this time, when he says, "While I'm gone, Joe is going to be at the helm," he takes two steps to his left, places his hand firmly on Joe's shoulder, and continues. "Look to Joe for help with any questions or problems. He'll be in charge."

Did the second scenario inspire more confidence in Joe than the first? Absolutely. Someone who witnessed the boss's hand on Joe's shoulder would be apt to feel more comfortable following Joe's lead than someone who did not. A simple touch made the difference. It usually does—if it's the right touch at the right moment. Had the boss ruffled Joe's hair or patted his cheek as he would a child's, his touch would have been inappropriate—and ineffective.

TOP PEOPLE KNOW HOW TO TOUCH

In fact, the higher up the career ladder you climb, the more important it becomes to "reach out and touch someone." It takes personal confidence to do that—and an understanding of when, where, and how to touch *appropriately*. Again, moderation and thoughtful, purposeful action are the key. Anything good can be bad when poorly timed, haphazardly executed, or taken to extremes.

Touch is as legitimate in a business setting as it is on an athletic field. No one objects when football players slap hands and pat one another on the back after big plays, or when baseball players hug the pitcher after the last out is made. Well, there is no reason not to give and receive appropriate physical support in the business world either.

When you want to congratulate, compliment, calm, sympathize, gain attention, affect, influence, or inspire someone, a touch can work wonders. You can do it anywhere—in a job interview, a job termination, a board meeting, or on a sales call—so long as you are consciously aware of and in control of your actions and confident and comfortable with yourself.

You can touch as frequently as it "feels right" and still not touch too much. My research indicates that most of us *should* touch more than we do. It creates a bond with others. And it feels good.

> "When I think of touching, I see it as being difficult to give, yet so satisfying to receive."
>
> —ROBIN MANGOS
> *Managing director, International Travelseekers*

Touch Gives Comfort and Shows Support

In company with various senators, ambassadors, and other prominent professionals, Bob Graves, founder of the National Marrow Donor Program, attended a dinner to honor a transplant recipient. The honoree, who happened to be a blue-collar dockworker, was clearly uncomfortable among so many high-powered individuals, and Bob noticed the man's uneasiness. He walked over, stood beside the seated man, and gripped his shoulder as a fellow dockworker would to show friendship. The recipient's tense shoulders immediately relaxed and he reached over to touch his wife's arm. She took his hand and they sat contentedly holding hands until he was called to the podium to receive his award.

Touch Can Influence

A well-known financier was approached by a young businessman for a loan. Although the financier decided that he could not lend the young man money, he offered to walk across the floor of the financial center with his arm around the businessman's shoulder. After seeing the two men together, a number of other financiers introduced themselves to the businessman, and one of them gave him the loan.

Touch Both Sexes Equally

"I met, spoke with, and touched every person in the room. It took a while, but it was worth it. When one man I work with caught me shaking hands and kissing a woman colleague's cheek and criticized me for being sexist, I kissed him on the cheek too."

—REUBEN MARK
Chairman, president, and CEO,
Colgate-Palmolive Company

In business, males can touch males, females can touch females, males can touch females, females can touch males, subordinates can touch bosses, and bosses can touch subordinates.

PLAN TO TOUCH

Don't wait for the emotion of the moment to strike you. Decide to touch more people more often—and follow through. Even write yourself a reminder, like the one a chief shared with me. It read, "Physically pat Jack on the back today."

And don't make the mistake of thinking you are the exception to the rule and that the ability to touch and be touched is not a necessary skill for you. No matter who you are (and no matter whom you touch), a touch that is *planned, purposeful, and tailored to fit the occasion* will leave a favorable impression, convey a positive message, and earn you just as much money while making your work environment far more enjoyable.

How to Touch in a Business Environment

1. Touch males and females the same way. Be consistent.
2. Be supportive, encouraging, or caring—whatever fits the situation. (Being condescending or sexually seductive is *not* the appropriate attitude for touching in any business situation.)
3. Because some people are more "touchable" than others and a few prefer not to be touched at all, you must be sensitive to the reactions of people you touch. An initial, planned "accidental" touch can help you test someone's receptiveness to being touched. For example, as you casually head toward the coffeemaker, lightly touch the other person's arm and ask if he wants his cup refilled too. Or when walking down the hall with someone and reaching

a doorway together, touch his elbow as you say, "You first." Observe that person's response. In most instances, he is apt to be surprised, but he usually won't be offended.

4. Don't sneak up from behind. Before making physical contact, make sure that the other person is aware of your presence. Stop and touch.

5. Plant your hand firmly on a hand, arm, or shoulder. (Touching an elbow seems most universally acceptable.)

6. Maintain physical contact for a split second.

7. Keep your hand still and steady. Do not stroke or pat.

8. Place your hand and remove it in an equally purposeful and definite manner. Don't be tentative or you'll look suspicious and unsure of yourself.

9. Smile, relax, and look as if you expect the other person to accept the touch in the manner you gave it. If you look as if you are worried about the response, the person you are touching is more likely to question your intent (or think he should be worried too).

10. If you simply cannot bring yourself to touch, at least make an extra effort to convey the message a touch would through your facial expression, tone of voice, and words. But doing this exclusively is gutless.

11. Practice, practice, practice. The ability to touch effectively and feel comfortable doing so, which many of us have lost, can be found again with practice.

A *word of advice*: Always keep in mind that touching, as I'm discussing it, works in our American business culture but may not work as well or be as acceptable in other cultures. Although when I asked the Japanese executive vice-president of a major automobile manufacturer if the Japanese minded being touched by American businessmen, he responded, "No, we are more Americanized now. We study Americans. Americans should have studied us."

TOUCHING THAT CAN CAUSE TROUBLE

The type of touching most likely to cause trouble is touching yourself. I'm referring to *men* who:

- adjust their ties;
- tug at their shirt cuffs;
- hitch up their belts;
- push up their eyeglasses;
- twist their mustaches;
- pull on their socks;
- play with their wedding rings.

And *women* who:

- fluff their hair;
- adjust their bra straps;
- fiddle with their jewelry;
- straighten their slips or pantyhose;
- rub their thighs;
- brush imaginary lint off their blouses.

And anyone, male or female, who chews fingernails, wrings hands, or scratches various body parts.

In the workplace, you'll see many low- and middle-level employees but few senior-level people touching themselves in the ways I just listed. Those touches are generally unnecessary, usually distracting, and more often than not nervous fillers. *Don't do them.* They rob you of your executive presence. When you do have legitimate cause to touch yourself (or simply can't resist the urge to scratch that itch), do it slowly and purposefully. You'll look less anxious and be less distracting.

THE BUSINESS HUG

"When I meet new people, I'll grab their hand, shake it, and give a bear hug by putting my other arm around their shoulder. Their reaction may be catatonic. They may try to take two steps backward. Or they may simply relax and enjoy it. But they don't forget it."

—JOHN KREBBS
President, J. Parker Company

Is it appropriate to embrace a business associate? Like John Krebbs and other chiefs I've interviewed, I think it is. Some relationships and some situations merit more than a perfunctory handshake. When your intention, attitude, and physical positioning are controlled and consistent, giving a hug is a memorable way to say hello, good-bye, thank you, and more.

Unfortunately, like any form of physical contact, your embrace *could* be misinterpreted. But the fear of being sexually harassed or accused of sexual harassment should not prevent you from hugging business associates. Instead, give that hug but control your actions to avoid giving off inappropriate signals or sexual innuendos.

1. Expect acceptance, but if in doubt, the first time you hug, say something along the lines of, "You've been so supportive, I'd like to give you a hug."
2. Grasp right hands and place your left hand around the person's shoulder, then lean your upper body toward him or her.
3. Turn your head so that your lips don't brush against the other person's check, collar, or lapel.
4. Hold the embrace a second or two longer than a typical handshake.
5. Don't touch pelvises.
6. Release the person from your embrace, look him or her in the eye, smile, and step back. Pause briefly and then re-

sume your conversation, exit, or do whatever else you were planning to do after the hug.

HOW TO RECEIVE A TOUCH

At a lecture given by public relations guru John Scanlon, I sat next to a CEO I had interviewed earlier in the day. Each time he wanted to make a comment, he placed his hands on both my shoulders, pulled me into his space, and then spoke. He used exactly the same actions with a gentleman seated on his other side.

As the man who calls the shots in a major corporation, that CEO would be considered intimidating by almost anyone's standards. But his touch was not intended to intimidate, and neither the man to his left nor I resisted or recoiled from it. We accepted the touch for what it was—an attempt to make it easier for one person to be heard by another—and were able to enjoy the CEO's witty commentary throughout the lecture.

A few minutes into the luncheon that followed my speech to the Young Presidents' Organization, the man seated beside me took his napkin off his lap, dipped it into a glass of water, reached over and swiftly wiped my white jacket lapel—removing the spot of gazpacho soup that I had splashed on it. Just as quickly, he returned his napkin to his lap. For a split second I was taken aback by his gesture and was about to rebuke him for "invading my space." Then I realized that he had listened to my talk and was, in his own way, taking the initiative, as I had suggested. As he would later admit, he was also testing to see just how I would respond. Fortunately, I followed my own advice, assumed that his gesture was well intended, and chose not to overreact to it.

It is as easy for us to misinterpret someone else's touch as it is for them to misinterpret ours. In either case, the misunderstanding and the adverse reaction that arises from it can damage a business relationship or start off any interaction on a sour note. To benefit from touching in a business setting, you must not only learn to give touch appropriately but also to *receive it gracefully*. Assuming that a sexual overture is not being made and that sexual harassment is not the other person's intention:

1. Don't act as if you've been zapped by an electric shock from a cattle prod. Don't grimace, glare, jump, or abruptly pull back as if you're having a repulsion convulsion.
2. Allow the touch. Be aware of it. Accept it. Or merely endure it if you are, for some reason, repulsed or offended by it.
3. Don't read ulterior meaning into a touch (unless the person reaches for your wallet or worse).
4. Lean into it.
5. If possible (and comfortable for you), reciprocate.

If you're on the receiving end of a business embrace, you should accept it as such and not read sexual overtones into it. But if you do not want someone to hug you, let him or her know. Be honest but pleasant about it. Make sure you give the other person an extra-positive handshake as a substitute.

In summary—in our WASPy, aloof, relatively impersonal culture it has become unfashionable to touch. That is unfortunate. But top people, people in the forefront, have the courage to touch anyway. They know that sometimes words are not sufficient. You must touch.

Yes, touching improperly can cause you major problems, but learning and practicing acceptable touching will help you avoid problems. So, please don't let a fear of PDA (public display of affection, taught as a taboo at West Point), sexual harassment suits, or AIDS keep you from touching. Do it, *but do it right.*

7

Good Posture—
The Healthy Way to Look Good

Right now. Stop and check your posture. Is your rib cage practically resting on your hips? Lift it. Are your shoulders slumped? Straighten them. Is your head tilted or bowed? Bring it to a level position. Breathe from your diaphragm instead of your chest. At first, this new positioning may feel uncomfortable. However, if you check yourself regularly and adjust yourself accordingly, good posture will become your natural posture.

1. *Good posture is energy gaining versus energy draining.* You appear younger and display the zest and energy top people look for when hiring or handing out promotions. (If there is a choice between two equally qualified candidates, the person who looks more awake, alert, and alive will get the position every time.)

2. *It actually improves health by ensuring that internal organs are in correct alignment.* Preventing a caved-in chest from collapsing lungs and causing circulation problems is just one such benefit. There are many others. In fact, an entire office furniture

industry has sprung up to meet the need for chairs and desks that promote good posture.

3. *Good posture enhances voice quality.* Because the full, unrestricted amount of air is allowed to flow up and out of your lungs, your voice becomes fuller, more resonant, and more powerful.

4. *You feel and look fit.* (And you look a good two inches slimmer around the waist.)

Poor posture makes you appear meek, mild, and weak. I've seen plenty of power suits and power ties on powerless-looking people. *It's not what you wear but how you wear it* that gets you to the top and keeps you there.

SUCCESSFUL PEOPLE CARRY THEMSELVES WELL

Chiefs don't have to tell people they are confident and successful, they show it with their posture.

> "My dad always demanded good posture. He was six three and seemed even taller when I was a young boy. He would come up from behind, place his hands on my shoulders and put my shoulders in position. I have him to thank for my good posture today. When you have good posture you stand well and look well; you improve your presence and even get your clothing to hang better."
>
> —**WINTHROP ROCKEFELLER**
> *Chairman and CEO, Winrock Farms, Inc.*

Good posture makes you look confident, successful, appropriately energetic—and taller. Statistics show that in this country, taller people make more money than shorter people in the same job. That is a form of discrimination no legislation can correct, and as a regional sales manager from a consumer products company learned, it can even prevent you from getting a job.

He said, "I was meeting with my potential boss. And because his boss was out of town and unable to meet with me in person, he called in to conduct a telephone-conference interview. My potential boss's boss didn't realize the speakerphone had already been turned on and thought he was talking only to the man interviewing me. I heard him ask, 'Is he six feet tall?' and the somewhat embarrassed interviewer glanced over at me and then answered, 'No, I don't think so.' The truth is that I *am* six feet tall, but I was sitting slumped in my chair and didn't look it. And I didn't get the job."

Good posture:

- sets a good example for your children;
- intimidates your competitors;
- gives your secretary and subordinates someone to look up to;
- makes your banker feel more confident that you'll repay your loan;
- and pleases your mother.

Most of us need to work on our posture—and it does take some work. I heard a movie star-turned-director comment, "I'd rather direct movies than act in them, because when I direct, I don't have to hold my stomach in."

How to Improve Posture

1. Maintain what Zen Buddhists call a posture action—as if walking with your head pushing the clouds away. Then relax into position.
2. When standing, keep your weight balanced over your center of gravity: feet solidly planted on the ground, legs slightly apart, and arms straight down at your sides as a West Point cadet does but a little less stiffly.

3. Keep your rib cage lifted off your hips, your head straight yet loose, your eyes level, your chin down and your stomach in. (Sorry, but you're going to have to hold your stomach in for the rest of your life.)

TOP PEOPLE "SEND OUT" ENERGY

Good posture gives you the energy to take your best shot at the top. Energy is the key to success in business and in life. *Physical energy* is required early on in your career. As mentioned in chapter 1, it gives you what it takes physically to perform your job. If you appear energetic and eager, show tenacity and stick-to-it-iveness, you're likely to be promoted to positions that require *intellectual energy*. In those jobs, you must prove that you have the smarts and the competence to do your job. The mistake most people make at that level is assuming that if they get smarter, they will be promoted. Not true. *Emotional energy* is also needed. Emotional energy makes you aware of how every aspect of yourself (from your posture to your presence) affects others. It is the source of your ability to effectively relate to people.

Whether you are sitting or standing, walking through corporate headquarters, or shaking hands with guests at a cocktail party, good posture helps you look as if you have plenty of energy under effortless control. I call that having *relaxed energy* (be it physical, intellectual, emotional, or all three). It comes from the obvious—good health, a well-balanced diet, proper breathing, good posture, regular exercise, sufficient rest—and the not-so-obvious—self-confidence, productivity, the sense of accomplishment you get from doing a job well, and from recognition.

One Sunday, Bill Farley, chairman of Fruit of the Loom, and I were in a town where one of his plants is located, and he decided to give me a quick tour of the operation. Since the plant was closed on Sundays, the only person there when we arrived was the security guard. Looking as if he were carrying the weight of the world on his hunched shoulders, he answered Bill's knock. But when Bill introduced himself and asked the guard for *his* permission to look around the plant, he straightened right up. Beaming with pride, he replied, "Certainly, sir." Then, after saying, "I'll bet you know this plant as well if not better than anyone," Bill Farley asked the guard to escort him through the plant. The man's posture improved even more. In fact, he looked four inches taller and so full of energy that he practically bounced as he took us on our ten-minute tour. By the end of it, he seemed like a new man.

Successful people send out energy. They don't "suck it in" the way people with frantic energy do. People with frantic energy are easy to spot. They belong to the "Excedrin and Diet Coke for lunch bunch" and count minutes as if they were dollars— brushing their teeth in the shower to save time, wearing a watch with an alarm set to go off every ten minutes to end every meeting, and walking in an overly-eager-to-get-there hunched-over position. They're draining to be around and have no staying power. Individuals with frantic energy burn out. Their careers go up in flames with them.

Conversely, people with relaxed energy have the stamina to work fourteen-hour days, solve complex problems, and effectively interact with the many people they encounter every day. They can and do make it to the top—and stay there. You will too if you strive for an appearance of relaxed rather than frantic energy in your physical presence. Good posture is a good place to start.

8

Stand Up to Be Counted

Designer Carolyne Roehm, president of Carolyne Roehm, Inc., is tall (nearly six feet in heels), and when she stands up, people can't help but notice her. Sometimes she stands and stands and stands, outlasting everyone else in the room in order to appear confident and in control. Others conclude that she is confident, even when she isn't. "I may be off, on edge, and wishing I could be somewhere else," she said. "But my sense of showmanship allows me to walk out purposefully, stand and smile."

Just like everyone else, top people don't always *feel* certain. But they know that with the right stance they can *look* certain. They stand more often than people at any other level in the corporate world.

TOP PEOPLE TAKE A STAND—LITERALLY AND FIGURATIVELY

They stand up when anyone enters or leaves a room or office. They stand up to introduce themselves and stand up in the presence of subordinates and senior personnel alike. They even instruct their secretaries to stand up each time someone comes through the door.

Once top people stand up, they frequently remain standing. I've attended many meetings that began with the participants on their feet and continued that way to the end. With little time wasted on chitchat, getting seated, or shuffling papers, decisions were made quickly, and all parties were able to get back to their own offices and their own tasks in record time.

Stand up! You'll stand out and:

- show respect;
- be courteous;
- feel energized;
- appear more youthful;
- let others know that a meeting or conversation is drawing to a close;
- seem more decisive (many decisions are made and most are finalized from a standing position);
- demonstrate an ability to "think on your feet"—a highly valued trait in the business world and one that will improve your chances of being promoted.

STAND UP FOR YOURSELF!

Even with so much to be gained, many people hesitate to stand up at all. They seem to feel that standing upright is too risky, that like a nail, they might get pounded. In reality, when you stand, you "stand up for yourself" and are *less* likely to get pushed around, shouted down, or walked on.

After I had made several unsuccessful attempts to schedule a meeting with a company president who was very busy, he finally agreed to a thirty-minute interview. He was very cooperative and informative, but exactly thirty minutes after I arrived and in midsentence, he stood up. Although he finished his thought, I didn't have to be told that no more words of wisdom would be forthcoming. By standing up, he made it crystal clear that when my time was up, it was up, and there was no point in asking for so much as another minute with him.

Like that of the company president, *your* stance can make an immediate, no-nonsense statement. It can say that you are confident, in charge, and someone to be reckoned with.

There is no cut-and-dried, one-size-fits-all right or wrong way to stand. However, some stances are more *effective* than others in a business setting. Generally speaking, these are stances you should *avoid*.

- Looking as though a thousand pairs of eyes are fixed on you and can see through your clothes. This nervous, borderline bashful stance includes rigid posture, a serious face, and hands clasped in front of you, covering your crotch like a fig leaf.
- A "cowboy" stance—eyes lowered, legs apart, pelvis protruding, thumbs hooked in belt loops and fingers curled toward the crotch.
- A "military cadet at attention" posture—ramrod straight, arms held rigidly at your sides, thumbs parallel to your thighs, and fingers curled, as if holding a roll of quarters.
- A "street gang member" stance—leaning against a post, wall, or doorway with your hands in your pockets and a sneer on your face.

Assuming any of the above positions diminishes your effectiveness. So does dancing around, fidgeting, and shifting your weight back and forth from one foot to the other. Stand still. If you show others that you can control your body, they'll see you as someone who is in control of his or her life and career.

How to Stand with Professional Presence

1. Maintain a relaxed, energetic posture with eyes and head level.

2. Assume a neutral or "ready" position with your arms loose at your sides so they are free to gesture. Keep your hands out of your pockets and do not cover your crotch or fold your arms across your chest.

3. Stand close enough to the other person to be personal, but not so close as to be intrusive.

4. Stand upright rather than leaning against a door, wall, lectern, or furniture. The former position makes you look solid and sure of yourself. You'll look uncertain and easy to sway if you lean.

5. Don't touch yourself or pick real or imaginary lint off your sleeves; smooth your clothing; tug at your waistband; straighten your tie; fuss with your hair; or rub your hands (like Lady Macbeth attempting to scrub off the "damned spot").

Finally, I strongly recommend that businesswomen stand as frequently and as readily as their male counterparts. Don't remain seated when someone comes into your office or joins you at a table—no matter what the old etiquette books say. If you want equal opportunities and equal treatment, you must literally and figuratively stand up like a man.

9

Sit for . . . a Lasting Picture

Now that you've reached this page and read the title of this chapter, I wouldn't be the least bit surprised if you were asking yourself, "Is she *really* going to teach me how to sit? Does it *really* matter?" Well, I am, and it does.

HOW YOU SIT CAN AFFECT OR DETRACT FROM YOUR PROFESSIONAL PRESENCE

Not long ago, I was watching an old cops and robbers movie, and in one scene the leading man entered a room to face a panel of grim-faced officials who were clearly prepared to leave no stone unturned during their interrogation. In other words, the leading man was about to be put on the hot seat and had every right to be nervous. But if he was, he didn't show it. He walked up to the straight-back chair that faced the panel, turned it around, swung his leg over it, and sat down, as if mounting a horse. Now, that may not be a move most of us will ever choose to make, but it certainly made a powerful statement and let the panel members know that the man they were about to interrogate was no pushover.

In my office, I keep two chairs pushed back from my desk to add space and make the room feel more open. When people come in for meetings, I'll say, "Pull up a chair," to let them know that they can move closer to my desk. They usually respond by pushing or carrying the chair forward to a position that is comfortable for them and then sitting down. But on one memorable occasion, a CPA I was interviewing about working for me walked over to a chair, turned his back to it, bent over in a hunched, semisquatting position, and curling his fingers up under the seat, pulled the chair behind him as he took little baby steps toward my desk.

Although it may not have been fair and it may have been an inaccurate reading of the CPA's abilities, I found myself thinking, "If this man can't handle this chair effectively, how can he handle my business?" But then as I've said (and whether it's fair or not), *people draw conclusions about you based on what they see*. You can control what they see. But that CPA did not. Unless he wanted to look incompetent (which is doubtful) or intended to move the chair no more than a few inches, he should have moved the chair before going to sit in it and not the way he did.

Sitting is one of those small, seemingly insignificant things that makes a big difference. A company president who had recently received a presidential appointment said this about his first meeting with President Bush: "Sure I was nervous, but I sat there [in the Oval Office] like I belonged there."

Executive presence is, in large measure, the ability to look as if we belong wherever we find ourselves. And the fact is that during most of any business day we find ourselves seated or sitting down or getting up from a seated position—at meetings, civic gatherings, job interviews, business meals, and in front of bosses, subordinates, peers, or competitors. People watch us sit and, based on what they see, draw conclusions about us.

Although we don't spend much time thinking about what we

might be revealing, others can tell from the way we sit whether we feel: nervous or relaxed; in control or flustered; competent or incompetent; comfortable or uncomfortable; confident or insecure. And they respond accordingly. Unless we control how we sit, how we get up, and how we position our bodies while seated, we rarely get the response we want.

SUCCESSFUL PEOPLE "RISE TO THE OCCASION"

Like so many adages used to capture people's characters, "rising to the occasion" originally described a physical characteristic—how someone with confidence and authority got to his feet when he became aware of people or circumstances that required his attention. It still applies to both attitude and action—and it is unlikely to be applied to people who seem to be bowing when they stand or who flop down onto a chair as if it were a bed. *Raise and lower* your body if you want to sit with professional presence and avoid being perceived as subservient or sloppy. Don't bow and flop.

How to Sit in a Controlled Manner

1. Approach the chair.
2. Pause.
3. Keep your upper and lower body in alignment to stay balanced.
4. Maintaining good posture, bend your knees and purposefully lower your body.
5. Sit on the edge of the chair first.
6. Then use your thigh muscles or hands to push yourself toward the back of the chair.

To stand up in a controlled manner, reverse the sequence. Once seated, place your upper body—specifically your arms— in an *asymmetrical* position. This can be done by:

- resting on only one armrest;
- putting one arm on the back of the chair;
- stretching one arm across to another chair or table.

With each arm doing something different, you automatically appear more relaxed. As a result, other people tend to be more relaxed in your presence and more receptive to your ideas. On the other hand, when your arms are symmetrically arranged (both doing the same thing), you'll look nervous—like a patient in a dentist's chair whose white-knuckled hands have a death grip on each armrest.

Watch other people or observe yourself in the mirror. You'll have no trouble seeing the difference between the effect of sitting asymmetrically and sitting symmetrically. (And you should have no trouble making up your mind to use the more beneficial position.)

To make a favorable impression while sitting, you'll need to control your legs as well as your arms. This is particularly crucial for women. It may sound sexist, but men can sit any way they want: legs apart, ankle over a knee, or knee crossed at knee. Women, who often wear skirts in business settings, must be more deliberate. The visibility of their legs can be distracting and may prevent them from making as favorable an impression as they would like.

A woman's best business choices for positioning her legs are knees, calves, and ankles together with ankles crossed or knees crossed. If she selects the knees-crossed position, she should make sure her calves and ankles are together in a straight line and *not* apart in an upside-down V. This not only creates a pressure point on the calf that can result in varicose veins, but also is all too often accompanied by a nervous bobbing or bouncing of the top leg. A woman who swings her leg up and down in that manner does not look controlled. She looks girlish and flirtatious. This may be fine under different circumstances, but it won't do anything positive for her if her goal is to be effective (and taken seriously) in business.

Although it may still seem as if I've gone into a lot of detail about a relatively trivial matter such as sitting, the knowledge and awareness you gain by effectively handling the little things and positively affecting others in small ways *builds confidence*. And that confidence enables you effectively to handle *any* situation. Small actions and minor details eventually add up to create a big picture—in this case, a finished portrait of you at the top of your field.

10

A Gesture Says a Thousand Words

Top people use purposeful hand and body movements to get their message across to others. They know that, like a picture, a gesture is worth more than a thousand words.

• Sirio Maccioni, owner of the renowned Le Cirque restaurant in New York City, is a master of running the show by using gestures as unspoken words. Like a basketball coach sending plays into the game from the sidelines, he coordinates the action in his dining room with hand signals. When his people see him gently slap the fingers of one hand inside the cupped palm of the other, they don't have to be told to move more quickly. They immediately respond to the sign for *pronto*. Sirio is so skillful in this area that he was asked to direct the seating at Malcolm Forbes's funeral just as he directs his restaurant seating—wordlessly.

• While explaining legal liability to his operations people, John Moore, president of Electro-Test Inc., gestured with his hands to portray a maintenance man climbing a ladder. By pointing to the corners of his mouth, he humorously showed lawyers salivating. Finally, he raised one arm, as if holding a checklist, and as he covered each point he used his free hand to check off that item on his imaginary list. Moore's gestures complemented his words. By showing as well as telling his audience what he meant, he got them to understand more in five minutes than the lawyer who spoke to them earlier and gave them three handouts had been able to in two hours.

Gesture—purposeful movement used to convey information or illustrate a point—is yet another piece in creating the picture of executive presence. Although we are predominantly verbal, there are times when only a gesture will do. In addition, our hands and arms can literally "paint a picture" to give our words more impact. Gesturing demonstrates *our* passion, enthusiasm, and certainty as well as captures *other people's* attention and maintains their interest in whatever we are trying to say.

When you gesture, you physically and productively release nervous energy. You also combat fatigue and "get your blood flowing," instantly energizing yourself. Gestures help the people listening to you understand your message more readily and remember it longer. (Research on television news viewers confirms this. Their retention increases when they see video footage pertaining to the story they are hearing, versus merely hearing the story read by a newscaster.)

• *Gestures sometimes say MORE than words and make it possible to respond to others more effectively.* For instance, a "thumbs up" sign, which conveys agreement, approval, congratulations, and enthusiasm all at the same time, has more impact than the words "great idea" or "go for it" would. And if you've ever watched a panel discussion, you know that the person who has the microphone is rarely the only one making a point. By shaking his head "no," the panelist three chairs over can convey his dissenting opinion to the audience—without saying a word.

• *They give you something useful to do with your hands.* You'll make a better impression than you would if you put your hands in your pockets, fiddled with your jewelry, or held on to a podium for dear life.

• *Gestures can improve voice quality.* Movement relaxes a restricted body, giving your voice more power and emotion. Try gesturing while on the telephone. You'll sound more enthusiastic. The other person will notice—and respond favorably.

In many professions, the ability to create visual pictures to accompany one's words is crucial. People who speak in public rely on gestures to capture and keep their audience's attention. Most politicians study what they call "purposeful movement to illustrate a point," and those movements usually include shrugs, nods of the head, lifted eyebrows, and tilts of the head, as well as hand gestures.

As I've mentioned previously, anything good taken to extremes can become bad. That definitely applies to gesturing. If your movements are random, abrupt, too stiff, too broad, or more a reflection of your anxiety than your message, they will be distracting, confusing, and damaging to the favorable impression you are trying to make.

For gestures to enhance (and not diminish) your professional presence, they must be well executed.

1. *Always use gestures that are appropriate for and acceptable in a specific situation.* Vulgar, gross, or profane gestures rarely if ever fall into that category! Also keep in mind that gestures meaning one thing (and having a positive impact) in the good ole USA may have a different meaning and effect in other countries. The A-OK sign (thumb and first finger together forming a circle with the remaining three fingers pointing upward) is one example. It is commonly used and universally understood in this country but has a very derogatory connotation in some Arabic countries.

2. *When using your hands and arms, keep them away from the rib cage.* Make sure there is daylight between upper arms and chest.

3. *Hold each gesture for a split second and try to make each motion as smooth as possible.* Rapid, jerky movement makes you look nervous, edgy, artificial, or like a tin soldier. Use one hand at a time to avoid looking like a windmill in high wind.

4. *Synchronize your words and actions.* Think of what you will say, show it, and say it. *Don't* think of what you will say, say it, and after the fact remember to show it.

Successful people gesture because they have the confidence to do it. Nervous, insecure people are so afraid to do something wrong that they don't do anything at all—and they don't get to the top or stay there. So, take the risk. Show what you mean as well as tell it.

11

Speech and Silence—
How to Use Both for Business
Success

As you move up through the ranks, you need to avail yourself of every possible tool to be more effective. Your voice is one of those tools.

Of course, like so many other details addressed in this book, at first glance the quality of your voice seems unimportant. "Does anybody truly pay attention to it?" you may wonder. Or you may be thinking, "I've made it this far without voice instructions, why should I worry about it now?" Well, I can assure you that even though very few people will come right out and compliment or critique your voice and even though you'll rarely get feedback on how your voice is affecting others, people *do* notice it.

• A female boss cornered me after a speech and told me that one of her female subordinates had been in the audience listening to me. "I hope she understood the significance you've put on voices," the boss said. "If she doesn't change her breathy, child-like whisper voice, I'm going to have to fire her."

• Though an up-and-coming financial analyst was due for a promotion, he didn't receive it. When his boss referred him to me for coaching, he attached a hand-scribbled note to his performance appraisal. It read: "Doesn't have an executive voice or laugh."

• On another occasion, I was brought into a company by the number-three man. He was convinced that the company president's voice was adversely affecting morale and explained, "He's doing an excellent job of running the company, but he speaks so softly and slowly that everyone thinks he's tired, uninterested, and unmotivated. It's demoralizing—and downright depressing to be around him."

YOU HAVE TO SPEAK UP TO STAND OUT

Others *do* notice voice quality and draw conclusions from it. The most common mistake people make in this area is the one the company president made. They speak too quietly and in a slight monotone, using what I call a "bored"-room voice. It is a safe, unobtrusive tone of voice but not always an effective or inspiring one. (For women in particular, it conveys a willingness to accept a subservient, second-class status.) Even so, most of us have no trouble justifying our soft-spokenness.

For instance, during a private conversation with that company president, I learned that he had almost been kicked off his high school football team because of his hyperactive behavior; that he had come within an inch of being dropped from a military pilot training program because of high blood pressure; and that at age thirty-nine, he had the first of two minor heart attacks. After the second, he resolved to slow down. He did not rush when walking, moving, or gesturing. And in keeping with his personal stress-reduction program, he talked very quietly, very calmly, and excruciatingly slowly. He was determined never to be uptight or physically pressured ever again. *His reasoning may have been sound, but his effect was detrimental to his colleagues and his company.*

Once he became aware of the demoralizing chain reaction his voice set in motion, the company president changed. Without altering his personal health objective, he modified his voice and learned to speak quietly or more loudly, slowly or more quickly, depending on the situation and what he hoped to accomplish. By replacing his "bored"-room voice with a boardroom voice, he restored people's confidence in him at all levels of the organization.

You too may think:

- "Using a quiet voice keeps me calm."
- "I don't want to be louder than life."
- "I'm big, so I have to speak softly to offset my size."
- "I'm soft-spoken with people because it's easier on them and less likely to lead to confrontations."

All of the above are good reasons for speaking softly some of the time—*but not all of the time.*

I am not telling you to abandon soft-spokenness altogether and use a raised, aggressive voice instead. Speaking in a loud, inflammatory, argumentative manner rarely invokes a positive reaction. A pleasant, assertive voice with a *variety* of speech patterns does.

The art of delivery is based on doing whatever it takes to be heard and understood at any given moment. At times louder is better. At other times quieter is better. Sometimes silence is best of all. You need to speak to your audience, speak entertainingly, speak with pauses. On occasion, it works best to talk faster. On other occasions, a slow, deliberate pace is most effective. The best general voice is an adaptable voice. Variety breeds interest, believability, and respect.

SPEAK UP TO FIT THE OCCASION

Top people use different voice qualities in different situations, changing their volume, pace, and inflection to suit their purpose.

They choose the best voice for a particular occasion or the one most likely to elicit a favorable response from a particular person. The result is clear, authoritative, and effective communication.

The fact is that very few of us actually speak in exactly the same way at all times. Most of us automatically change the tone, inflection, speed, and volume of our voices in response to different people or circumstances. Without giving it much thought, we alter our speech patterns to make similar words sound very different when speaking enthusiastically to a college friend, resentfully to an ex-spouse, seductively to a prospective spouse, respectfully to a minister, or angrily to the neighbor whose barking dog kept us awake half the night. By increasing your conscious control over something you already do naturally, you can increase your executive presence (and the effectiveness of your voice in business settings).

DEVELOP AND USE AN EFFECTIVE VOICE

Although you've talked for most of your life, your present use of your voice is not the only way you can talk comfortably. With a little effort and a few simple changes, you can develop a voice that helps you better control how you affect others. The first thing you must learn (or relearn, since you were born knowing how to do it) is how to *breathe* correctly.

Proper Breathing

"A few years back, I started having throat pain and went to a doctor who told me that I was irritating my vocal cords when I spoke because of shallow breathing. After he pointed that out, I noticed that my father and son breathe and talk the same way— incorrectly. And after I followed the doctor's advice to change my breathing, I not only got rid of my throat pain, but also discovered that when I'm conscious of my breathing, I have a more effective speaking voice."

As that CEO found out, even though breathing is something we do to exist, we don't always do it with maximum effectiveness. Because of nervousness, tension, fear, or stress we tend to constrict and restrict our bodies and our breathing. Over the years, we have *unlearned* something we knew how to do as babies—breathe naturally. *Most of us no longer breathe as deeply or as slowly as we should.*

1. Take out a watch with a second hand and, breathing as you usually do, count how many breaths you take in one minute (each inhale *and* exhale equals one breath). The typical total is about seventeen breaths per minute.
2. Now, "sigh out" to become more aware of your breathing. Exhale and let out as much air as possible. Then, without slumping your posture, relax your stomach muscles to inhale. You will notice the natural refilling of your lungs. Repeat this deliberate breathing several times until you're in the slow, steady rhythm of a rocking chair, back and forth, in and out.
3. Count your breaths while doing this more deliberate (and natural) breathing. You should discover that the number of breaths you take has been cut almost in half. Generally speaking, when you breathe properly, you do not exceed eight or nine breaths per minute—and you feel much more relaxed, yet energetic.

Practice and get into this good breathing habit. It increases the flow of oxygen to your brain, may improve the thinking process, and:

- relaxes muscle tension;
- reduces nervousness;
- calms your spirit and your mind;
- improves circulation;
- reminds you to relax your facial expression;
- improves your voice quality;
- and as a two-time heart attack victim put it, "gives you

something constructive to do while you count to ten before blowing your stack."

When you breathe deeply as described, you avoid shallow throat breathing and strain, which can cause you to lose your voice or speak breathlessly at a higher pitch and sound scared. Instead, you'll be breathing from the abdomen with your diaphragm pushing air up and out. As a result, you'll be able to project your voice from the center of your being and have a much more positive, powerful impact on others.

How to Use Your Voice Effectively

1. *Aim for variety.* The same two speech texts delivered aloud will be judged differently based on the variations in voice quality used by the speakers. The speaker with more vocal variety and flexibility will be more favorably received. So, strive for versatility. When the situation calls for a hard line, an intellectual approach, or a soft touch, speak like a tough guy, a professor, or with a smooth and easy tone. A monotone is perceived as boring, suspect, and insincere.

2. *Relax your jaw and tongue.* As you read this, your jaw is apt to be firmly clenched. It may not feel tight or tense, but just try to wiggle it from side to side. Difficult isn't it? A relaxed jaw would move more easily. Although a "set jaw" may be considered manly, a relaxed jaw improves voice quality. Because the jaw muscle is proportionately one of the strongest muscles in the entire body, if you've gotten into the habit of keeping your jaw tight and tense, you'll have to "retrain" it. When you are listening, reading, driving, or thinking, practice consciously relaxing your jaw muscles.

3. *When you speak, use your entire body.* Your voice functions most efficiently and comes across most effectively when it has the full cooperation of your mind and body. Concentration enables you consciously to control your volume, pace, tone, and inflections. Your facial expression, posture, and gestures enhance the effect of anything you say. If you consider the message you wish to deliver and then add purposeful movement to it, you have a physical game plan and are more likely to create a favorable impression. Naturally, you'll need to breathe properly.

4. *Start each new thought with a new breath of air and save enough breath (or take another breath) to end your thought with power.* Please note, that I am *not* telling you to make one breath of air last for an entire thought. If you try that, chances are that you'll run out of air before you finish and your voice will fade away, taking the thought with it. Most of the time, you'll want to complete your idea at the same voice level you started it, even if you vary your tone and volume in between. Starting the thought with a new breath and saving enough breath or taking another one toward the end of your statement enables you to do that.

Sometimes it will be more effective to begin quietly and build, so that the ending gets more emphasis. When the most important part of what you have to say is at the end of the sentence, don't let it fade into oblivion.

A good place to work on this technique is with your voice mail or answering machine. Listen to your incoming messages. You'll notice that many of them fade away at the end. Don't allow yourself to fall into that trap. Pay attention to how those fading messages sound and learn what *not* to do. Then listen to your outgoing message. If it fades off, rerecord it with a stronger ending. Even when leaving a message, you can set yourself apart from the rest.

5. *Don't mistakenly conclude that the increased volume resulting from breathing properly and relaxing your jaw is too loud.* After visiting the dentist and getting a shot of Novocain, most of us feel as if our lips and cheeks are puffed out like balloons, but other people can't even see the swelling. The same distorted perception accompanies the breathing and voice changes I'm recommending. So, give yourself time to get used to your new boardroom voice. Ask a friend or colleague to listen to you speak and stop you when you get too loud. Then start talking, and with each new thought, get louder. You'll sound too loud to yourself much sooner than you will sound too loud to someone else.

Obviously, you don't want to be loud and obnoxious, but you do need to be loud enough to be interesting—and heard. Try not to forget that your normal volume (even with proper breathing and a relaxed jaw) may not be loud enough for certain listeners—the hearing impaired, for example, or anyone listening in a noisy environment. Adjust your voice accordingly.

Occasionally, you may want to turn up the volume even further. For example, when one executive I interviewed was "a little uncertain" about a point, he made it louder than the rest. "And when I'm not sure how to pronounce a word, I say it loudly too," he explained. "People never question me." Although I am not necessarily advocating that technique, it does seem to work for that executive. He rarely appears timid or uncertain. What I *am* advocating is being aware of the impact made by various voice qualities, including volume, and selecting the ones that work for you in a given situation.

6. *Don't speak too hurriedly.* Gordon Parker, chairman, president, and CEO of Newmont Mining Corporation, has a very deliberate speech pattern. When I asked him about it, he explained, "People listen more carefully if they think you are thinking when you speak." I tend to agree with him. Even though people can hear two to three times faster than we can talk, most of us could stand to slow down when we speak. Hurrying makes our words seem less important and gives the impression that we do not think our ideas deserve more than the briefest amount of airtime. We appear to be rushing to finish so that someone with something more valuable to say can speak. Slow down. Allow for some pauses, some silence. People will listen more closely and have more respect for what they hear.

Don't slow down too much, however, especially if you are

speaking in front of an audience. Although an extremely fast speaker may frustrate listeners who can't keep up with him, an extremely slow speaker can bore and lose his or her audience.

7. *Face the person to whom you are speaking.* This courtesy should be extended to everyone. Don't speak from behind people or turn your back to them. If you need to talk to someone who is across the room, get closer before you speak. Speaking too loudly across the room makes you look rude, obnoxious, and insensitive.

8. *Gesture.* As explained in the previous chapter, people understand your message more readily and remember it longer when you gesture. In addition, the physical movement helps to relax your body and improve your breathing.

SILENCE IS GOLDEN

Both what you say and *what you don't* gets you to the top. Successful people know that. In fact, it seems as if the further up the corporate ladder they go, the fewer words they use.

As one CEO explained it, you maintain an executive presence by "talking little, saying a lot when you do, and telling others no more than they need to know." To be effective you must know how to speak as well as how and when to remain silent.

Unquestionably, many of us have a great deal of difficulty keeping our mouths shut. Some of us get nervous and feel compelled to fill up every gap in a conversation. Others feel rushed and try to cover everything we want to say nonstop in the limited time we believe we have. Or we may not want to look like we need a lot of time to think and, as a result, respond very quickly—sometimes without giving our response *enough* thought. But most of us have simply developed a bad habit of talking too much. To be as successful as you want to be, you'll have to break that habit.

Remaining silent does not mean refusing to participate, contribute, or communicate. Silence in a business setting does not involve angrily or impulsively clamming up. It is not giving someone the "silent treatment," as spouses or sulking teenagers have been known to do. It *is* purposefully being quiet, deliberately listening, and consciously choosing not to speak unless you can accomplish more with words than without them.

When properly used, silence:

- adds to your presence and mystique;
- minimizes mistakes;
- gets others to speak and allows you to learn more from what they say;
- gives others center stage when such a strategy is needed;
- enables you to control the direction of a conversation by choosing not to comment on topics you'd rather not discuss.

By remaining silent, you also:

- feel calmer and more peaceful;
- make whatever you do say seem much more important;
- demonstrate self-confidence, self-assurance, and self-control;
- sidestep escalating confrontations in which both parties say too much or say things they will later regret;
- clearly convey that you have "said your piece."

At the end of any day, most of us can recall at least one comment we wish we had not made. By learning to keep quiet, we can cut down on self-recriminations and worry less about the damage our hasty or inappropriate comments may have caused. Instead, we'll be able to recall the flip, poorly timed, or ill-advised remarks we did *not* make and gain confidence in our ability consciously to control our speech and silence.

As you practice "holding your tongue," remember that sometimes as much is said with silence as with words. Indeed, saying nothing can be one of the most effective ways to convey something. When you are silent people *really* listen to you—and they realize that you are listening to them.

Listening

"The most important discipline I've acquired since college is listening."

—JEFF SMULYAN
Owner, the Seattle Mariners

Top people listen more than they talk, and when they listen, they *really* listen. They know that the only way to have an effective dialogue with someone is to listen *effectively*.

Effective listening involves more than making eye contact and keeping your mouth shut. As you no doubt know, you can do that and *look* attentive without actually being attentive. Instead of concentrating on the message being conveyed, your mind wanders—back to a meeting that just ended, ahead to an upcoming social engagement or to what you'll say as soon as the speaker stops to catch his breath. By allowing your attention to be diverted, you not only run the risk of missing important information but also leave a less than favorable impression on the person with whom you are conversing.

To listen effectively:

- Pause.
- Silence all internal dialogue. Let extraneous thoughts pass through your mind without dwelling on them or allowing them to take your attention away from the speaker.
- Look at the speaker with a relaxed, open facial expression.
- Occasionally nod or say "uh-huh."
- Encourage the speaker to continue by saying something along the lines of: "tell me more," "anything else?" "keep going . . . this is interesting (or valuable)."
- Control your body language and facial expressions so that you do not look bored, intimidated, or intimidating. Any-

thing you do to make the speaker nervous or self-conscious will put a damper on the conversation and prevent you from getting all you could get from the exchange.

- Resist the temptation to jump in and speak your piece as soon as the speaker pauses to take a breath.
- Repeat what you hear—for clarity. This does not mean parrotting the speaker and playing back his message word for word. Paraphrase or briefly summarize the point(s) you believe he made and give him an opportunity to clear up any misunderstandings. You might even want to ask, "Is that what you meant?" or "Am I understanding you correctly?"
- When appropriate, later in your conversation, refer back to something that was said earlier. This reassures the speaker and conveys a message everyone likes to hear—"I was listening to you and what you said was important enough for me to remember."

INTERRUPTIONS

There's little doubt that frequent interruptions can distract and annoy a speaker as well as disrupt the flow of communication. However, taking the initiative to interject your ideas into a conversation is not all bad. Sometimes interruptions are actually interactions—a way for you to participate in the discussion. When properly timed and sparingly used, they let the speaker know you are listening and interested in what he or she has to say. They may even be greeted with a sigh of relief by someone who is rambling and digging himself into a hole.

It is acceptable to interrupt someone who is blatantly dominating a conversation or meeting. In fact, interrupting that person may be the only way you'll get a word in edgewise. It is also reasonable to interrupt when a lot of ground is being covered and you don't want to lose an idea that has occurred to you at a specific point in the conversation. In that situation you might say, "Let me cut in here for a second because you triggered a thought I may forget if we go on to another area." The speaker will usually understand.

In general, be patient and wait for a pause (no one can talk nonstop forever). And if you catch yourself interrupting inappropriately, immediately apologize and give the speaker the floor once again.

If you are the one being interrupted, you can:

- tolerate the interruption;
- ignore it;
- raise your voice and talk over it;
- nonverbally convey that you'll give the other person the floor as soon as you complete your thought (holding up your index finger or giving a stop sign with your hand are two gestures that effectively serve that purpose);
- verbally ask to finish making your point (I recommend touching the other person's elbow or shoulder to reassure them that you are not miffed and then interrupting the interrupter to say, "Let me complete this thought," or "I'm not finished yet").

One interruption can be considered an accident. Two or three within minutes is apt to be an attempt to get the upper hand or irritate you. Select your response accordingly.

II

FIT IN—THE ART OF RELATING

12

People Skills—
How to Fit In to Get Ahead
and Follow to Lead

Top people *stand out*. By using the techniques described in the first part of this book, they set themselves apart from the crowd. But they also *fit in*. Top people get to the top by appearing to belong there and effectively dealing with whomever they meet along the way.

"The most important asset a manager has is people. You have to have good people around you. Everything else you can buy or lease. My achievements are less a reflection of what I did alone than the result of my ability to orchestrate a team of people. I do that by delegating, giving plenty of rope and yanking the rope every once in a while. I praise people in a crowd and discipline them alone. If you cultivate people and treat them with respect, they'll do the job for you and be loyal to you. That's why, when I went from Avis to Hertz, then back to Avis, more than fifty people went with me each time. The excitement of business and what makes it tremendously satisfying for me is that I work with a wonderful group of people."

—JOSEPH V. VITTORIA
Chairman and CEO, Avis, Inc.

"It's impossible to avoid interactions with other people. I have to collaborate with them. I need their talents as well as my own. I can't plant the grapes, run the tractor or press the grapes alone. Everything involves working with and getting the best out of people and that requires a passion for what you do coupled with doing it well. You motivate the people around you with your attitude. It's infectious."

—TOM JORDAN
Owner, Jordan Vineyards

"The boss is the personification of the company. How people are treated by management is how the same people will treat customers."

—REUBEN MARK
*Chairman, president, and CEO,
Colgate-Palmolive Company*

These comments from three top people clearly support the point made at the very beginning of this book: *No one becomes successful or accomplishes anything of lasting significance without effective people skills.*

No matter how ambitious, capable, clear-thinking, competent, decisive, dependable, educated, energetic, responsible, serious, shrewd, sophisticated, wise, and witty you are, if you don't relate well to other people, you won't make it. No matter how professionally competent, financially adept, and physically solid you are, without an understanding of human nature, a genuine interest in the people around you, and the ability to establish personal bonds with them, you are severely limited in what you can achieve.

"You can have the smartest people in the world working for you, but if they can't communicate with and motivate other people, they are of no use to you!"

—**THOMAS BICKETT**
President and COO, Witco Corporation

When asked during dinner conversation why one of two people with comparable qualifications makes it to the top and the other doesn't, Tatsuro Toyoda, executive vice-president of Toyota Motor Corporation, replied, "Personality." He went on to explain that the one who would succeed would be the one who could get along with people. "A small difference can make a big difference," he said.

PEOPLE SKILLS

1. *These skills are not tricks or tactics for controlling or manipulating people.* They are techniques for controlling the effect you have on others. When you control your effect, you are more effective, more productive, and more in tune with the people around you—and they get along better too. As Tom Jordan said, your attitude is infectious. And your efforts to bond with and relate to others *as people* pay off more than any manipulation or control tactic ever could.

"If you create an environment where people are treated correctly, they will always give a full effort."

—**JOHN M. RICHARDS**
President and COO, Potlatch Corporation

2. *It's not just a matter of affability or popularity, gregarious backslapping or people-pleasing charisma.* Being likable is an asset, but you can't coddle people or back away from necessary confrontations for the sake of being liked by those you lead.

You'll lose your effectiveness. People respect a boss who "tells it like it is."

> "A CEO cannot be nice at all times to all people. He needs a strong inner core, clear values, a clear point of view. He needs high tolerance for mistakes but not tolerance for lying, dishonesty, covering up, or stepping over the core values of the company. It's hard for a leader to lead unless he's strong. But that doesn't mean he can't also motivate, inspire, praise, coach, and bond to build the team."
>
> —TIMOTHY DAY
> *President, Bar-S Foods Co.*

3. *People skills cannot conceal incompetence or be used as a substitute for basic knowledge and ability.* However, if you have taken the time and made the effort to establish bonds and relationships with others, they tend to be more willing to forgive your mistakes and give you second chances to show them what you can do. For instance, an accountant, one of his former clients, and their wives were dining together prior to attending a concert. Their amicable, freely flowing conversation made it apparent that they had enjoyed similar evenings together before. However, midway through their meal, when the topic changed to business, discussion revealed that the accountant had proposed a $50,000 budget for the last project of the client's he bid on, and the client had found someone to do it for $4,500. Despite being almost taken to the cleaners by the accountant, the client still had an excellent rapport with him— one which the accountant had nurtured, using people skills. Consequently, it was no surprise when the client turned to the accountant and said, "By the way, I have another project for you to bid on. Just try to be more reasonable about your fee this time, would you?"

You need people skills to get to the top and you definitely need them to stay there. The higher up the corporate ladder you go, the more important personal bonding and people skills become. *Management jobs are people skill jobs.* You can't manage people without having people skills.

TO DEVELOP PEOPLE SKILLS, EMULATE SUCCESS

Anything you do to bond with, build the confidence of, or bring out the best in your employees, bosses, peers, competitors, lawyers, doctors, children, spouses, customers, advisers, or anyone else is a people skill—and the more people skills you have the better. How do you develop them? You can start by emulating the positive attitudes and behavior patterns you observe in people who are already where you want to be.

> "Keep a keen eye trained on those who are successful. See how they operate. Discern their good traits from the bad. Tuck away and remember what you've learned by watching and listening. Then use it when you are in a similar situation yourself."
>
> —LAWRENCE WEINBACH
> *Managing partner-CEO, Arthur Andersen & Co.*

Although some chiefs have personalities or temperaments that have earned them a reputation as "born leaders," most leaders had to learn how to lead. They accumulated knowledge and technical skills through their formal educations. Then they developed their more intangible (and, in the long run, more important) interpersonal skills through hands-on experience and by observing successful people in action. They studied how leaders presented themselves, carried themselves, spoke, tackled problems, and much more. They incorporated whatever impressed them into their own repertoires. At every level of the corporate world they occupied, chiefs fit in by taking on the attitudes and actions that suited their status, position, and purpose. To get ahead in your chosen field, you must too.

To be the best, look for good examples and have the good sense to follow them. When job hunting, seek out a good job *and* a good boss. Two or three years down the line the allure of big money will fade. Hot projects will turn cool. Attractive perks will be taken for granted. But a good boss will have made a lasting impact on you and your career, teaching you what you need to know to be a good boss yourself someday.

Identify potential role models—people who are successful (personally as well as professionally), respected, intelligent, ethical, and admired. They can be superiors, colleagues, clients, customers, acquaintances, even people you'll never meet personally but can learn from nonetheless.

Sometimes you'll be fortunate enough to find role models who will also serve as mentors, actively guiding your career and sharing the wisdom they gained through their own experiences—as the chiefs quoted in this book are doing. Most of them had at least one mentor along the way. Few got to the top entirely on their own. So don't mistakenly assume that asking to be taught or wanting to learn from others is a sign of weakness. And don't sit back and wait for an invitation to be mentored. Identify someone you could learn from. Approach that person and once he takes you under his wing, stay in touch with him directly, personally, and continuously.

Emulating success does not mean becoming a carbon copy of someone else or pretending to be someone you're not. Playing a role or putting on an act will not get you very far. Eventually others will see through you. Your credibility as well as your rapport with superiors and subordinates will be lost.

Fitting in to get ahead *is* a matter of being open to new experiences, being aware of other people's actions, being sensitive to the effect of their actions, and choosing to engage in behaviors that you have seen working for others. There is nothing new or unusual about that. You have been doing it all your life.

From early childhood onward, each of us consciously or unconsciously emulates other people's values, work habits, attitudes, manners and mannerism, posture and comportment, facial expressions, speech patterns, and a host of other behaviors. The examples we follow either work for us and become part of our makeup and personalities or do not suit us and are discarded. The same principle applies to emulating the successful people we encounter in the business world. Adopt the attitudes and behaviors that will make you more effective—but still allow you to be yourself.

Once you have identified people to emulate:

- Closely observe what they do and say.
- Select the behaviors you want to emulate.
- Begin to reflect those behaviors. Think of yourself as a mirror image of your model and replicate the words and actions you have witnessed.
- Practice the new behaviors, paying close attention to their effect. Realize that anything new will feel odd and uncomfortable at first and use the response you get from others to help you learn what does or does not work for you.
- Keep using what works until it becomes second nature for you. The actions you are emulating start out as techniques, but with repetition, they become integral parts of you, enhancing your executive presence and your self-confidence.
- Finally, employ the observation and reflection skills you develop while emulating success to help you adapt to specific situations and fit in wherever you go.

EMULATE THOSE YOU HOPE TO AFFECT

Most of us naturally adapt ourselves to the people and circumstances we encounter. We automatically and often unconsciously adopt the posture, gestures, colloquialisms, speech patterns, and even the accents of people with whom we are conversing. An effective executive presence is based on consciously and purposefully doing what we already do naturally. We must knowingly and appropriately emulate those we hope eventually to influence, direct and affect. We must tailor our attitudes and actions to suit the occasion—not to be artificial, superficial, or condescending but to fit in, show respect, and connect.

When you're talking to a toddler, you crouch down to the child's eye level, speak in simple sentences, and use words you know a two- or three-year-old will understand. To avoid frightening or intimidating him and to improve your chances of getting through to him, you emulate the child with whom you are speaking. *You form a bond with him by becoming like him.*

In the business world, similar methods produce similar results. By actively observing the people with whom you are interacting and deliberately replicating selected mannerisms, speech patterns, attitudes, feelings, or actions, you:

- put them at ease;
- establish common ground and let them see how you are like them;
- build trust, rapport, and confidence, creating the bond that will eventually put *you* in a position to lead and enable *them* to accept your leadership.

HOW TO LOOK LIKE YOU BELONG

Your attire is one simple and effective tool you can use to create a bond with others in the workplace. In recent years, the trend has been to dress to impress and stand out rather than to connect and fit in. It is a widely accepted practice to wear clothes that make you look wealthy, successful, and even intimidating. As one CEO put it, "I dress to scare my staff." However, that approach is not always in your best interest.

A lawyer who was giving a speech to a group of executives gathered at a ski resort in Colorado wore a suit and tie even though his audience was casually attired in ski sweaters and boots. When I commented on his very businesslike appearance, he snapped, "At my fees they deserve a tie!" Hoping to convey his power and importance, that lawyer *emulated his perception of success*. Like people who buy homes in the "right" neighborhood, acquire the "right" car, or join the "right" country club in order to establish the "right" reputation, he thought his suit and tie would impress his audience and give his speech more impact. In reality, most of those executives—who were enjoying the opportunity to combine business with recreation—saw the lawyer as stiff and inaccessible and felt that his speech was dull and of little use to them.

While there are certainly times when your power suit and power tie (in this year's power color) will serve you well, if your goal is to build rapport and stimulate confidence in your ability to lead effectively, *I recommend being dressed and groomed in a fashion similar to that of the people you want to serve or affect*. When Mr. Big goes out onto the factory floor to talk with his workers wearing his custom-made suit, silk shirt, and a pair of imported shoes that cost as much the average machinist makes in a month, he'll be lucky to get more than perfunctory, one-word answers to his questions—no matter how amiably they are posed. But if he takes off his suit jacket and rolls up his sleeves, he'll almost always find his workers more receptive to his attempts at conversation.

Keep in mind that when people first look at you, they will notice what you are wearing. However, whether your goal is to stand out or fit in, remember that your attire is just one aspect of your executive presence.

- Don't be an empty suit. Clothes don't make the person. If you can't back up your "look" with substance, expertise, or style, you'll "get in over your appearance" and leave others with an unfavorable impression of your abilities.
- Don't let clothes become an obstacle, creating a distraction that detracts from your initial impact. Watch out for jangling jewelry, rumpled raincoats that you have to remove before taking your seat, short, tight skirts, and so on.

- And don't dress to emulate those you hope to affect when doing so would contradict what they already know about or expect from you.

"A Wall Street lawyer I know was trying a case in rural Michigan and originally planned to dress to fit the people and the environment. But an older and wiser lawyer stopped him. 'The judge and jury will know you're from a large firm,' he said. 'You'll be introduced as a lawyer from a New York law firm and they'll expect you to wear your three-button suit and vest. If you walk in with a blazer and slacks, they'll know you dressed down for the local yokels and be insulted. It will hurt your case, not help it.' "

—JOHN ZIEGLER, JR.
President, the National Hockey League

From the way you dress and the words you choose to your tone of voice and facial expressions, your emulation of others must be subtle and suitable to the occasion. I don't want you to copy, blatantly mimic, or mock others. I do want you to fit in and get "in sync" with those you hope to affect. They will accept you more readily. And only after they accept you can you start to lead. Once you do, others start emulating you.

Emulating those you hope to affect is just one of the many people skills you will use on your way to the top as well as after you get there.

A Few More People Skills

1. *Be open and approachable.* With your attitude and physical presence, invite people to approach you and talk with you. Take the initiative. Break the ice. People won't forget.

2. *Seek out those who seem hesitant to talk with you.* Although your natural tendency may be to talk with people you already

know and feel comfortable with, you must also approach new people—the friendly as well as the unfriendly—to get ahead in business. Don't justify keeping your distance with the rationale, "They have the personality of a rock. I'll never get through to them. So, why bother." You set yourself apart from the crowd by approaching them anyway. Besides, your assumption that people are "cold" could be off the mark. You may be misreading their signals. Approach them and see what happens. You are likely to discover that they were nervous or feeling out of place.

3. Carry on conversations and show that you are interested. Whether you initiate a conversation or others seek you out, talk, ask questions, appear interested, encourage them to tell you more. You'll establish a rapport.

4. Listen. (Don't react immediately. Listen.) Others sense that you are sincerely interested in them if, and only if, you shut up and listen. When you do respond, zero in on something they've just told you and get them to tell you more.

> "Top people must be straightforward, open, and friendly. They create an impact by being self-possessed yet willing to listen and focus on others' interests."
> —W. RICHARD KERN
> *Managing partner, Heidrick and Struggles, Inc.*

5. When appropriate, take action. During any conversation, if you make a commitment to someone, be sure to follow through on it. Don't make empty promises—not even seemingly innocuous ones. If you aren't going to "do lunch sometime," mention them to someone you both know, get back to them with the phone number they requested or send them your annual report, don't tell them that you will. To demonstrate your sincerity you must take action. Otherwise you destroy the trust and rapport you've worked so hard to develop. Few people readily trust new relationships in the first place. If you abuse someone's trust by not following up on a commitment, you'll rarely get a second chance from that person.

6. *Begin to bond in your own backyard and nurture your relationships with everyone everywhere at all times.* Mend fences internally. Practice your people skills on the people closest to you. It's all too easy to forget that the people with whom you already have relationships also need your attention, encouragement, and respect. So build allegiances and a strong base of support as well as hone your people skills by treating the people you know with the same humanness and consideration you would extend to someone with whom you are trying to create a new bond.

7. *If a choice has to be made, treat your subordinates better than you treat your boss.* Your success (or failure) depends on the performance of those you supervise. Use your people skills to motivate them. Otherwise, you'll demoralize them.

When you use people skills, you set the tone for others and lead by example. More than any other skill, people skills are observed and copied by the people around you. When you provide a model of fair treatment, sincere interest and personal effectiveness for others to emulate, you and the entire organization benefit.

One of the most important responsibilities you assume as you move up the career ladder to positions of leadership is being an effective role model for others. Just as you got ahead by mirroring those above you, the people below you will mirror your behavior once you are the boss. If you don't like what your subordinates are doing, look at their role model—you. And if you want them to do something, you do it first.

> "I always go up to the marketing floor and make a point to show myself, to eat in the cafeteria, to let people know I don't believe in extravagant luxuries like big black limousines. Whatever I do, others watch. I have

to set the example. If I spend money like a drunken sailor my people would too."

—ROBERT BALDWIN
Chairman, The Lodestar Group

8. *Do your best to care genuinely about and take an interest in people.* Sincerity and positive regard are two things that just can't be faked, and you need both to deal with people effectively. If you truly dislike all people and prefer not to deal with them at all, ever, then I suggest you work very hard on finding a cure for cancer. That is the only kind of professional success you can achieve without relying on people skills, and only after you've achieved it can you actually get away without personal bonding.

In the next few chapters, I'll be elaborating on some of the points I have just made and describing several additional people skills in detail—beginning with the art of relating person-to-person rather than role-to-role.

13

Get Personal—
How to Have Person-to-Person
Business Relationships

Whether you are a banker, an elevator operator, an art director, a computer programmer, a lawyer, or a window washer, you are also a person; human issues such as health, aging, money, personal happiness, and family matter to you. They matter to chiefs too—and the people around them know it. You may not be privy to the details of chiefs' personal lives, but *you can sense their humanness.* They get to the top (and stay there) because they are able and willing to get personal with their professional associates—subordinates, peers, and superiors alike.

BUSINESS IS A SERIES OF PERSON-TO-PERSON RELATIONSHIPS

Top people understand that life is a series of interpersonal relationships and that business is just a series of interpersonal relationships with money attached. They deal on person-to-person terms with anyone, at any level, under any circumstances because it enables them to form bonds readily, affect others positively, and conduct business successfully.

Person-to-person business dealings do *not* require you to get intimately involved in people's private affairs. They do not give you permission to "take things personally," reacting to every slight or rebuff with an emotional outburst. To get personal, you do not have to "spill your guts," and you should not get others to open up so you can take advantage of their vulnerabilities. Communicating on a person-to-person level *is* recognizing and addressing the human feelings, attitudes, preferences, and perspectives you have in common with your clients, customers, bosses, and underlings so that you can establish positive, effective working relationships with them.

How Do Top People Get Personal?

1. *Create a relaxed, friendly work environment.* Ronald Unkefer is the chairman and CEO of a California appliance/television/electronics store chain that he named the Good Guys because "our focus is on the customer, and customers want to do business with good guys." Unkefer extends his personal touch to customers and employees alike and apparently is a fun-loving guy as well as a "good" one. Although his office walls are decorated with the usual framed photos of company achievement award ceremonies, they also display photo after photo of serious-looking people in suits with cream pies dripping down their faces. In keeping with a long-standing company tradition, a pie-throwing free-for-all can be expected to break out before every photo session.

2. *Being visible and available—in person.* Joseph V. Vittoria, chairman, and CEO of Avis Inc., regularly takes grueling trips to as many as five cities a day for three or four days in a row. "I want to make sure my employees don't lose sight of me," he explains.

3. *Convey your thoughts and feelings to others in writing.*

"I send out lots of 'atta-boy' letters. It takes me only minutes to do it, but putting praise down on paper means a lot to people. I've even gone into their offices and seen congratulatory notes from me framed on their walls. I know I value the personal notes I've received. I have a little security box at home, and whenever I purge that box of old papers, I always leave two letters inside. One is a letter of commendation from my Corps of Engineers job thirty years ago and the other is from the number-two man at ITT, where I was a senior engineer over twenty years ago."

—GEORGE SAFIOL
President and COO,
General Instrument Corporation

4. *Allowing others to see more than your serious, businesslike persona.* Bill Daniels, chairman of Daniels Communications, has a magnificent home where he sometimes holds executive meetings around his kitchen table. He'll ask the participants to join him when he takes a break to feed the family of squirrels that live in his backyard.

5. *Reveal enough about yourself to make others feel comfortable in your presence.* John Green, president and CEO of Great-West Life Assurance Company, was addressing a group of seven hundred people, some of them due to come up onstage to receive awards. Sensing their nervousness, he began his speech by saying, "I can still remember the first time I talked in front of all of you. I was so nervous that my knees were knocking together. You couldn't see them behind the lectern, but I was sure the microphone would pick up the sound and you'd hear them."

With his little "confession," Green relaxed his audience and related to them *personally.* Instead of presenting himself as aloof, alien, and unapproachable, he revealed a facet of himself *as a person* (and not just a president or CEO). As a result, he connected with his audience and invited them to *have a relationship with him.*

Successful individuals know that people prefer to follow leaders who are human, approachable, . . . and have the courage to expose their own humanness as well as address the humanness in those around them. Most of us do not. We shy away from person-to-person business dealings because we believe that:

- we have to be impersonal to lead effectively;
- getting to know and relating to people personally wastes time, especially when there are so many more concrete and "useful" tasks we could be accomplishing;
- the personal information we reveal could be used against us;
- people really aren't interested in how we feel or what is happening in our lives or anything else that isn't directly related to our job descriptions;
- we will end up offending or alienating people by becoming *too* personal.

Some of us are so reluctant to get personal that we won't "speak from the heart" unless we are blitzed. The person to whom we are revealing ourselves is usually blitzed too, limiting the impact of our personal revelation—if it gets heard at all. The day a beverage company vice-president spent entertaining an important customer is a case in point:

> "We played golf, went to the Super Bowl, and finished the day with a nice dinner. The entire time we were polite but private. The reserve was never broken. Only during dinner, when we both had too much to drink, did we loosen up. Then we became buddies and, believe me, we didn't just talk about business. Without the drinking, we never would have gotten up the nerve to relax and be ourselves. It's too bad it took booze to do it. I don't want to get drunk every time I need to get to know someone."

Whatever the reason, the sad truth is that in business settings, most of us deal role-to-role rather than person-to-person. We bark orders at office managers and ream out copy machine repairmen without giving a second thought to how our harsh treatment affects them. We complain that our bosses are in "one of those moods" without knowing enough about them to sympathize with the circumstances that brought on their mood. We get right down to brass tacks with customers who, for all we know, may have just been diagnosed with a terminal illness or won the lottery. Some of us will nod "good morning" to the same security guard for ten years without ever knowing his name or work for the same company for two decades while maintaining the same formal professional façade. That's easy—and safe. But it also reduces productivity, creativity, and enthusiasm in the workplace.

When you stay in your role and deal with other people as if their roles are all there is to them, you seem stiff, boring, unapproachable, and somewhat suspicious. Just think about the impersonal bosses you've had. Did you trust them, feel comfortable seeking their advice, look forward to seeing or hearing from them? Were you motivated to produce for them? Probably not (and they probably have not advanced in their careers as steadily as more personal and personable individuals).

IT PAYS TO GET PERSONAL

From the day you enter the business world until the day you retire, you will have to deal with people. You sell to, buy from, court, criticize, hire, fire, instruct, and receive instructions from *human beings*. Just as you or I do, they wake up in the middle of the night tormented by their insecurities . . . think their financial peaks won't last and their financial valleys won't end . . . play practical jokes on their friends . . . favor their mother's chili over that of any restaurant . . . love bargains and shop at discount stores, even though they can afford to pay full price

. . . struggle through divorces . . . worry about balding . . . fear being fired . . . get rebuffed by the opposite sex . . . have children who get in trouble . . . write poetry . . . clean the garage on Saturdays . . . suffer bitter disappointments . . . count their blessings . . . complain about sore backs, meddling in-laws, and paying taxes but still would not "switch their problems with anyone else."

Those personal experiences and emotions are universal. No matter which job titles we have or how much money we earn, on a personal level, our similarities outnumber our differences. If you remember that and connect with people on that level, you'll find that:

1. *Others react more favorably to you.* Because they haven't expected you to point out something you have in common with them or reveal a bit of personal information to them, they are pleasantly surprised. And more important, they immediately feel closer to you and more receptive to whatever you have to say. (Think about it. Don't you feel that way when someone makes a personal connection with you?)

2. *People more readily open up to you.* Your openness gives them the confidence and courage to reveal themselves too. As you continue to communicate on a personal level, you invariably discover more common ground on which to build a positive working relationship.

3. *You learn not only about others but also about yourself.* There are few experiences that compare to hearing your own thoughts come out of someone else's mouth or realizing that someone else is grappling with the same feelings or problems that are baffling you. You feel an instant affinity for that person— as I did when one of the chiefs I interviewed said, "I'm one of the luckiest doofuses in the world." (A line I have used myself.) You also gain insights that can help you grow, change, and become more effective personally and professionally.

4. *You build trust.* People follow and support individuals they trust, and they are more likely to trust someone who appears human, approachable, and willing to reveal his own imperfections. Your subordinates, peers, and superiors don't put their trust in you because of your role, position, or title. They grow to trust you because you let them see who you really are and show them that you are interested in them as people.

5. *Your subordinates will be more productive and enthusiastic.* Getting personal motivates employees, reinforcing their perception that management cares and will listen to their concerns. "He makes me feel important," a woman who worked for Joseph J. Melone, president of Equitable Life Insurance Company, explained. "The people who work here *are* important," Melone said when I relayed that comment to him. "If I'm not paying attention to what's on their minds, I'm not doing my job."

In addition, person-to-person business dealings give people personal recognition, which is something all of us—even the very successful and accomplished—thrive on. I can still recall how the late Dr. Armand Hammer, chairman and CEO of Occidental Petroleum Corporation, beamed when he told me how Mikhail Gorbachev concluded a speech by introducing his Russian audience to "the best businessman from the United States" and then walked into the crowd to embrace Dr. Hammer. No matter how big you get, a "personal touch" still has a powerful impact.

Getting personal also reduces tension, makes you seem less intimidating, creates a relaxed, cordial work environment, and "breaks the ice" during the first few uncomfortable moments of any interaction.

A top salesman for a computer resaler called on a new customer who had sounded stiff and unreceptive on the telephone and was proving to be a "tough nut to crack" face-to-face. Noticing the Minnesota Twins cap on the customer's coat rack and other Minnesota Twins paraphernalia around his office, the salesman decided to take a risk. "I have to show you something I think you'll appreciate," he said. Then he stood up and reached inside his slacks. Grasping the elastic waistband of his boxer shorts and explaining that they were a present from his wife, he pulled his shorts out far enough to show his customer the Minnesota Twins logo printed all over them. Both men laughed, relaxed, and began talking baseball, forming a bond that made the business discussion that followed all the more pleasant, productive—and profitable for the salesman.

Yes, person-to-person business dealings *are* risky. Although you need not be as gutsy as that salesman, in order to reap the rewards of being personal, you *will* need to take the risks and find the courage to get personal. If you don't, especially after others have made the first move, you'll create mistrust, indifference, and resentment—which certainly won't take you to the top or keep you there.

How to Get More Personal

1. *Work on your own attitude.* Become more willing to deal with others personally and begin looking for common ground. Remember that the personal—feelings, fears, likes, dislikes, pastimes, families, humor, and so on—is universal. There is always some point on that level where you and another person can connect.

2. *Reveal enough of yourself to show that you are human.* I'm not talking about "gut spilling," "emotional flashing," or sharing your deepest, darkest secrets. Telling a humorous anecdote, admitting an error you made earlier in your career, recounting a nerve-racking, slightly embarrassing, or otherwise memorable incident that your current situation brings to mind, or simply mentioning something your wife, son, mother, or dry cleaner said is enough to demonstrate your humanness—and get a person-to-person conversation going.

3. *Ask questions.* Listen; give others an opportunity to talk about themselves.

4. *Respect the other person's privacy with confidentiality.* Keep what you hear to yourself and don't bring it up at a later date to gain some sort of advantage over that individual. Getting personal is *not* a technique for manipulating others. It is a way to build trust, rapport, and effective working relationships.

5. *Be consistent.* Person-to-person business dealings rely on actions as well as words and are most effective when your overall management style is relatively informal. Without being casual, sloppy, or laissez-faire, your attire, office furnishings, meeting locations, visibility, availability, and interest in calling people by their first names (and having them use yours) can demonstrate your humanness—and sincerity. If you turn your personal approach on and off like a faucet or, after twenty years of cold, impersonal behavior, waltz in with a big smile on your face and call everybody by his or her first name, you will seem phony and be suspect.

6. *Realize that abandoning role-to-role dealings and replacing them with person-to-person communication cannot be accomplished overnight.* Start small and move slowly. Get some practice—at the next business-related social function you attend, for instance.

GETTING PERSONAL AT BUSINESS PARTIES

The further up the career ladder you climb, the more business-related social gatherings you'll have to attend. Rather than promoting personal interactions, these supposedly social events bring out some of the stiffest, most insincere, and boring behavior you'll ever see. A typical conversation goes something like this:

"How's business?"

"Fine, and yours?"

"Fine." [Silence as both parties stir their drinks or survey the room.]

"How's next quarter?"

"Good." [More silence.]

"How's the wife? And kids?"

"Great." [Both have been glancing around, looking for an escape route. One spots someone he has to "catch up with."]

"Well, good to see you."

"Yes, good to talk to you too."

"Let's do lunch."

"Fine. Great. I'll give you a call." [Neither party believes that, and they go their separate ways to have virtually identical conversations with dozens of other guests with whom they have socialized on countless occasions—but never gotten to know personally.]

That sort of interaction is so commonplace at business parties because most of the people who attend them are accustomed to dealing with one another role-to-role, and those who would like to get more personal tend to be nervous and uncomfortable. Social situations stir up insecurity under the best of circumstances. When future business dealings (and money) are involved and you have few if any personal ties with your fellow guests, anxiety levels skyrocket. The trick is to realize that everyone else is probably at least as nervous and uncomfortable as you are. If you take the initiative and get personal to make things easier for others, they'll notice, appreciate it, and get more personal too. You could go one step further and actually enjoy yourself.

Here's how:

1. *Expect acceptance and accept others as well.* Almost everyone, at every professional or social level, is more worried about being rejected than interested in rejecting you.

2. *Position yourself near the door.* That way you get to talk to a lot of people for a short amount of time.

3. *Regardless of how well known you are, if others are wearing name tags, wear one too.* Without it, others may think you are too important (or arrogant) to approach or get to know. Although the natural tendency is to pick up a name tag with your right hand and place it on your left lapel, wear yours on the right lapel. That makes it easier for others to read your name while shaking your right hand.

4. *Say your first and last name while shaking hands with each new person you meet.* The more well known you are, the more important it is to volunteer your name. It makes others feel important.

To remember names:

- listen for them;
- repeat them right then;
- use them in your conversation;
- write them down when you have the chance;
- if you forget, introduce yourself again (because they've probably forgotten your name too) and listen for theirs again, remembering it this time.

5. *If you would walk up to a man and shake his hand, do the same with a woman.* Although old-fashioned etiquette says "wait until the woman extends her hand," in any business-related setting, you need not hesitate to shake hands with women.

6. *Carry your drink in your left hand.* This way your right hand is free to shake—and it isn't cold and clammy.

7. *Maintain a friendly, approachable facial expression.* At a social gathering you never know who is watching you, who is going to know you, or who is about to talk to you.

8. *Maintain good posture.* You'll look more confident.

9. *Initiate conversations.* People you already know or people standing alone should not be the only people you approach. People at the bar or in groups are "fair game" too.

10. *Both volunteer information about yourself and ask questions to uncover common interests.* Feel free to talk about religion, sex, and politics. (Remember: the most personal is also the most universal.)

Here's a good sequence for talking with an unfamiliar person:

- reveal something about yourself;
- ask a question and listen to the answer;
- reveal something else about yourself that is related to the answer;
- then ask a follow-up question and listen.

By getting others to talk, you relax yourself and reduce their tension. They will be grateful to you for "breaking the ice."

11. *Plan ahead.* Always bring a few jokes or humorous personal anecdotes to business parties. If you get people laughing, they can't help but feel comfortable with you.

12. *Follow up on any commitments you make during your conversations.* Most people don't—which is why we feel that party talk is insincere and artificial.

13. *Carry business cards.* You can give them to people when you want to cut off the conversation but not the person.

14. *Treat your spouse or escort as well as you treat your "business acquaintances."* Neither ignore them nor overdo the affection. The key to being personal in a business setting is consistency.

IS IT POSSIBLE TO BE TOO PERSONAL?

Absolutely. You want to be personal but not inappropriately intimate, cordial but not a pushover, interested without being nosy or intrusive, and informal enough to be accessible while maintaining some sense of order and propriety. Many of the chiefs I interviewed mentioned the balancing act that person-to-person business dealings require:

> "I'm very personal and tend to associate personally with employees. But we all know very well where pleasure stops and business starts. A hammer can come down as easily on friends as on anyone else."
>
> —ALVAR J. GREEN
> *Chairman, president, and CEO, Autodesk, Inc.*

> "I establish a contract among employees that we will laugh a lot, not take ourselves too seriously but take our work seriously. I want them to be comfortable and I need to be close enough to them to know their problems—or else how can I help then? But I do set parameters for myself. I deal amicably and sincerely without invading their privacy or allowing them to invade mine."
>
> —W. TED WRIGHT IV
> *Managing director, The Regent of Sydney*

> "I want my employees to know me well and even know my wife. And I want to know them and their wives. You can judge people by how they treat their families. The patterns they establish in life are the same ones they'll establish in the company. That's why I want nonbusiness relationships to exist. But I'm always aware of the fine line between being personal and getting too personal. I don't know how to describe it, but I know where it is and I don't cross it."
>
> —JOSEPH V. VITTORIA
> *Chairman, and CEO, Avis, Inc.*

Like these top people, you'll have to use your smarts, your instincts, and your experience to show you know how to get personal without being too personal. Obviously, you'll know not to ask someone you meet at a business cocktail party, "Do you bathe with a sponge or a washcloth?" But in other instances, the line between appropriate and inappropriate personal contact will be more difficult to discern. One particularly fuzzy area these days is office romance. In case you're wondering, let me tell you in no uncertain terms—*that is NOT what I mean by being personal!*

Office romances:

- have destroyed entire companies;
- can devastate individuals, families, and children;
- impair your decision-making ability and cause others to question or reject the decisions you do make;
- are likely to cost at least one party his or her job (with the lower-level person usually being asked to leave the company);
- damage morale;
- may result in legal action;
- cause others to lose respect for the individuals involved;
- almost always cause some sort of disaster.

No matter how you look at it, when two people who work for the same company become romantically involved, someone (and all too often everyone) loses. So, *don't fool with the help.* There is no gray area. It's black and white.

If you see an office romance starting, do something to prevent it. When you notice two people hovering over a desk together or off in the corner giggling, interrupt. Face the problem head on. Address it. Do what you can to stop it before it starts.

If approached, don't become involved. Just say no. Don't do it. Voice your displeasure. The first time someone initiates an intimate contact, say something like: "I don't like what you're doing."

The second time: "This is the second time you said something like that. I don't like it. I'm not interested and I want you to stop."

The third time: "I've told you once. I've told you twice. This is the last time I am saying it—NO!"

If there is a fourth time, don't say any more! Seek professional advice.

If you are involved in an office romance, get out of it. Don't promote the person you're involved with and don't make the mistake of thinking it's "innocent" or that you won't get caught. Eventually, you will. There are no exceptions to the rule.

Most top people, once they've made the decision to go for the top, end all inappropriate private relationships. They know that having an office romance is not being "human." It's courting disaster.

14

Fit In to Get Ahead—
Through Story-Telling

Dave Fanning, president of GTE Customer Network, is tenacious, goal oriented, and hard working. Now, he could have just told me he had these qualities, and I probably would have believed him. But he found a more memorable, impressive, and credible way to reveal himself. He told the following story:

As a teenager, Dave eagerly looked forward to the day he would drive, and, as his sixteenth birthday approached, he asked his father when that day would be. His father said, "When you have a driver's license, a car, and insurance. You have to have all three."

So Dave went to a local dealership and found a '52 Chevy that was selling for $120. When he learned that the dealer wouldn't sell it to a minor on a payment plan without a parent's cosignature, he negotiated a deal. "I'll pay you twenty dollars cash a week and you can keep the car until I finish," he offered, and the dealer accepted the arrangement. Using the money he earned by working at a bowling alley, Dave made his payments, got his driver's license, and on the day his last payment was to be made, took a bus to the car dealership and proudly drove home.

When Dave's father saw the '52 Chevy parked in the driveway, he asked, "What's that?"

"That's my car," Dave replied. "I paid for it."

"Do you have insurance?" his father inquired. Since Dave did not, he was told, "Then your car stays in the driveway until you do."

For six weeks the car sat there. Dave's buddies brought him gas in five-gallon cans, and he went through two tanks of gas just sitting inside and listening to the radio. He washed and polished the car's exterior so often that it practically needed a new paint job by the time he'd saved up enough money to pay for his insurance. But he persevered until he had accomplished his goal.

To this day, whenever Dave Fanning sees a two-tone '52 Chevy, he fondly recalls his first car. And when I see one, I think of him, the story he told me, and the kind of businessman he is. His tale made a more powerful and lasting impact on me than his merely stating "I'm tenacious, goal oriented, and hard working" ever would have.

TOP PEOPLE TELL STORIES

Although the shortest path between two points is a straight line, sometimes the direct, matter-of-fact route is not the best one to take. You are more interesting to others (and better able to relate to them) when you speak colorfully, concretely, and episodically. Top people know that. They use anecdotes, examples, and illustrations as tools to:

- convey their humanness, form bonds, and build rapport;
- help others understand their ideas more quickly and remember them longer;
- make conversations livelier and more entertaining;
- highlight important principles, clearing up and driving home their intended messages with everything from their

own experiences to parables from the Bible or the teachings of Buddha;

- support their claims, facts, and opinions with believable examples;
- recognize and subtly compliment their peers, superiors, or subordinates, making them look and feel good by relating positive stories about them to others;
- allow others to extract the point from a story and draw conclusions for themselves rather than being told what to think or how they should view an issue. Instead of being spoon-fed information, listeners participate in the communication process and feel that they "own" the ideas being presented to them. People are always more willing to "invest" in and support ideas they feel they helped to generate.

There are countless times during any business day when stories can be used to help you communicate more effectively. In job interviews, for example, people are often asked to comment on their strengths and weaknesses. Most people say something like, "I work well with people," when they could paint a more telling word picture by saying, "I've been told I work well with people and in my most recent position, it was a good thing I did. I inherited a creative team that didn't get along well at all. In fact, they couldn't seem to agree on anything. So, I met with the leaders of each group to discuss their objectives, problems, and desires. Then, after I spent some time sorting out what I heard in those meetings and drew some conclusions, I brought the group leaders together and shared my conclusions. To everyone's surprise, they all agreed with me. After some nervous laughter, a camaraderie started to develop and the group leaders continued to meet on a regular basis. Today, they are the smoothest operating team in the organization."

In addition, using stories to illustrate your points is particularly beneficial when you are talking to the press. Reporters want interesting copy. The more tangible, practical examples and anecdotes you supply, the better equipped the newsmen will be to capture you, your project, or your ideas on paper. With practice you will be able to get your point across in a two-paragraph press release or a two-minute telephone interview for a newspaper or magazine article, a thirty-second version for a television interview, or even a ten-second version for a radio sound bite.

How to Tell a Telling Tale

1. *Draw from your own experiences*. Start a personal story collection by taking some time to think through important times in your life and how you would make them clear to someone who wasn't there or didn't know you well. *List twenty-five or thirty interesting events that have occurred in your life already*. These could be business accomplishments (how you landed your first job, made a notable sale, got to meet an important person), family folklore (how your father reacted to the accomplishments I just mentioned, the lawn-mowing service that was your first business venture, the advice your grandmother gave you along with her spare change), school or church experiences, or the lessons you learned through your involvement in the military, sports, and so on.

Using a separate sheet of paper for each experience, *write a detailed description of*: the situation you faced; the action you took; and the result.

Make sure your tales make an important point or illustrate things you did that others might not have done. Revise or replace anything that others might react to with a resounding "so what."

Then boil down your page of details to a paragraph. Finally, trim the paragraph down to a sentence or two while still covering the three areas listed.

2. *Constantly add to your personal story collection*. Interesting things happen to you all day long. Jot them down and use them in any situation they seem to fit.

3. *Keep a file of stories*. By either writing them down or keeping them in your memory, make a file of stories you've read

or heard that made an impact on you and could have a similar effect on others.

4. *Use descriptions.* When telling stories, use descriptions that incorporate as many senses as possible. You might *hear* your grandmother's gravelly voice, for instance, or *feel* the hairs on the back of your neck standing on end, *see* the fire in someone's eyes, *smell* the boss's Old Spice aftershave preceding him down the hallway, and so on.

5. *Be personal.* Whenever possible speak to the human emotions and universal conditions that people generally have in common. Remember, you aren't telling a tale to hear yourself talk but to communicate and bond with those who are listening to you.

6. *Vary the length of your anecdotes and make sure any story you tell gets to its point quickly.* You don't want to earn a reputation for going on and on and on.

7. *Inject humor whenever and wherever you can.* Humor provides you with yet another avenue for conveying your humanness, bonding with others, and fitting in to get ahead.

15

Fit In to Get Ahead with Humor

"If you're going to ask people to make a commitment
to work long hours, travel, and so on, you have to have
fun as a key item on your agenda. Levity, laughter,
and a sense of fun bring out the best in people. If
the workplace becomes miserable and not fun, you
can't generate the kind of energy and enthusiasm you
need."

—ALEX J. MANDL
Chairman and CEO, Sea Land Service, Inc.

Never underestimate the value of having fun while you work.
Fun is one of the most powerful motivators around. An atmosphere of good cheer stimulates creativity. It increases productivity. What's more, an optimistic attitude and the ability to
laugh at yourself from time to time make you easier to relate
to personally—and professionally. You seem more human and
approachable to your superiors, subordinates, and peers.

FUN CAN BE PART OF DOING BUSINESS

When preparing the corporate culture statement for Contel Customer Support, Inc., the tenth and final point David Fanning listed was "HAVE FUN!" His subordinates will tell you, "He does."

Many large, successful companies (Hewlett Packard, Apple, Ford, Chrysler, to name a few) would not exist today if their founders had not been having a good old time working on projects in their garages. Unfortunately, as such companies grow bigger and bigger, fun begins to fall by the wayside. The need to compete, excel, avert disasters, and keep an eye on the bottom line has all but silenced the sound of laughter in modern office buildings and factories.

Nowadays, many of us can't even imagine ourselves "lightening up" and having fun in a business setting. We're afraid to let down our defenses. Or we mistakenly think that levity isn't professional and will prevent us from being taken seriously. Although it's true that you can communicate clearly, advance in your chosen field, and even make a lot of money without using your sense of humor or having fun, your trip up the career ladder is apt to be more rapid, interesting, and enjoyable if you do.

Top people laugh. A sense of humor separates them from the also-rans. The chiefs interviewed for this book are living proof that finding your niche and getting ahead in the corporate world need not be serious business all of the time. In fact, they seem determined not to take even the most confounding situations they face *too* seriously. Their philosophy is: "If you can't change it or accept it, you might as well laugh about it." And they laugh a lot.

During the summer of 1990, when arson fires caused millions of dollars worth of property damage in Santa Barbara, my friends Kathy and Peter Mackins lost their home. "We wanted to clean out the closets, but this is ridiculous," Peter said to Kathy as they surveyed the burned-out ruins of their dream house. And seeing that the only thing standing was a door frame with the dead bolt mechanism still intact, as they walked away, he quipped, "Be sure to lock up before you leave, dear."

Laughing in the face of adversity makes troubles more bearable. Laughter also reduces negative tension and replaces it with a positive physical reaction. It is, as the saying goes, good medicine, getting your blood flowing as your heart rate increases, exercising your stomach and facial muscles, and producing a general sense of well-being.

"In certain situations, I'm going to laugh or I'm going to cry, and I consider crying a waste of body fluids," Winthrop Rockefeller, chairman and CEO of Winrock Farms, Inc., explains. "When the going gets tough, you can use alcohol, drugs, or humor. I choose humor." Top people usually do.

The use of humor is so prevalent among chiefs that almost all of them have something to say about it. John Butler, president of Financial Programs, Inc., gets people to laugh "because I don't want them to drag me into a rut. Besides, most people I know look better when they're smiling."

Other chiefs mentioned that humor:

- "breaks down the barrier of awe between bosses and subordinates";
- "furthers camaraderie";
- "helps me stay sane";
- "strips away pretensions and gets to the heart of any matter";
- "masks the bite of my criticism";
- "makes me look like a good Joe."

They believed that a bit of levity:

- "enables me to dodge unanswerable questions";
- "permits me to attack without leaving footprints";
- "helps people forgive more easily and say to themselves, 'Maybe, he's not as bad as I thought' ";
- "breaks tension";
- "lets me laugh an issue out of existence";
- "cements relationships";

- "is like a splash of cold water that refreshes and recaptures others' attention during a meeting."

They rely on humor to:

- "perform small acts of rebellion in pompous corporate settings";
- "maintain control of the situation";
- "keep me healthy; we Italians have a saying—a good laugh makes good blood";
- "keep things from getting boring";
- "make sure my kids don't grow up to be stuffed shirts."

LIGHTEN UP!

To bring more fun and laughter into the workplace, you do not have to put a thumbtack on your boss's chair, tell locker room-type sex jokes around the water cooler, or slap colleagues on the back and say, "Did you hear the one about . . ." I'm not suggesting that you become a stand-up comedian or collect cartoons.

Humor that helps you to fit in to get ahead is reflected in your attitude as well as in your actions. It demonstrates that you have enough self-confidence to laugh at yourself from time to time and enough sensitivity to put others at ease by commenting on the lighter side of what seem to be dead serious situations.

Naturally, you'll want to use your common sense and good judgment. Generally speaking, wearing a Groucho Marx nose, mustache and glasses is not a good use of humor for business. But don't be overly cautious. You will never please everyone, no matter what you do. Just try not to make jokes at someone else's expense or continue to make light of an issue when you can see that your attempt at humor is angering another person.

As a rule, *stay away from a style of humor that is insulting, hostile, or otherwise likely to leave a negative impression.* Putdowns, sarcasm, caustic comments, and ethnic jokes may work for Don Rickles or Joan Rivers and they may even get you a few laughs at a business cocktail party. But they will work against you in the long run. When what you are about to say is something you'd resent if it happened to or was said about you, *don't say it!*

That should be a given, but sometimes in your effort to be humorous, you may miss the mark. It happens to the best of us:

> "Although I used to use ethnic humor and poke fun at others, I've made a concerted effort to change that. The other day, however, I slipped. As I was leaving the bank, I noticed that one of the personal bankers was apparently doing very little. I made a flip comment about her inactivity—not meaning to be negative. But the banker took it that way. I walked across the street, bought a small box of candy, went back and gave it to her with my apology. Now when I see her, she greets me with a smile rather than the scowl I might otherwise have received—and deserved."
>
> —ERNIE HOWELL
> *Retired president, St. Regis/WPM*

Like that chief, if you unintentionally offend or hurt someone with your levity, stop and right then and there apologize. You can mend a fence and get your relationship back on a positive track by humbly acknowledging your faux pas and saying something like, "I'm sorry. I was trying to be funny, but what I said was inappropriate."

To cultivate a sense of humor for (and about) business, be aware of your effect and don't be afraid to apologize if you cause ill feelings. Then you can:

1. *Feel free to develop your own style.* The only requirement is an attitude of optimism and good cheer—a sense that the playing field of life is not tilted against you. An ability to laugh at life and at yourself is helpful. However, not taking yourself too seriously is not enough to make your business dealings more human and more fun. Neither is waiting for opportunities to laugh to occur spontaneously. If you want humor to happen, you must take the initiative and make it happen with one-liners, quips, anecdotes, word plays, visual humor, voice changes, or any combination of these that suit you. Observe other people's humor, identify the things you like, and try them yourself. Practice and incorporate whatever flows most easily into your own repertoire.

2. *Listen to what's being said and what isn't, then comment on what you've heard (or haven't).* Some of the best business humor comes from the odd, ridiculous, or even anxiety-provoking things that are constantly happening in the corporate world.

A vice-president of sales was selling a multimillion-dollar software package to a Jamaican hospital. He had "back-doored" his way to the top, sidestepping the man whose name would go on the contract, and that man was in turn delaying the closing of the deal. The VP had left for Jamaica with instructions from his boss to "get over there and get that order signed."

The meeting wore on and on, and still no signature seemed to be forthcoming. Finally, the VP said to the customer, "This is like going to the prom. Two months ago, I got up my nerve to ask you. You accepted. I worked part-time jobs so I could rent a tux and a limo and buy you dinner. Now, the day before the prom, you tell me you're not going. Can't you see that I've been waiting a year to try to have my way with you."

The analogy captured the customer's attention. The humor reduced tension in the meeting. The risk resulted in success.

"You should have asked me one more time before you rented the limo," the customer replied. Then he signed.

Long reception lines, people hovering around a celebrity hoping to catch his eye, board members sitting in tense silence waiting for the chairman to arrive, phones ringing repeatedly or at inopportune moments, elevators that seem to take forever to arrive, all present opportunities to exercise your wit—and make a connection with humor. It's a matter of timing. You have to have the presence of mind to pay attention to what is going on around you and the courage to comment on it. As Lucille Ball once explained to a reporter who asked how she got to be so funny, "It's not that I'm funny. I just have guts."

3. *Expect acceptance.* It's risky to bring levity to the workplace and anxiety provoking to consider the prospect of injecting humor into your business dealings. You're likely to catch yourself thinking, "Maybe I shouldn't say that," "Maybe it isn't appropriate," or "What if they don't think it's funny?" However, if you censor yourself or wait for permission to use your sense of humor, chances are that you'll miss an opportunity to make a connection—or worse.

A telecommunications consultant who was pitching his firm's services to a new prospect found his potential client so aloof that he abandoned his usual warm, humorous approach. "I decided to get more professional," the consultant told me. "I was as cool as he was because I thought that's what he wanted." But that proved not to be the case. The prospective client decided not to go with the consultant's firm, explaining that he "liked to deal with consultants who are fun."

Although you may indeed be disappointed if you expect your attempts at levity to be greeted with laughter (or applause), you can safely assume that most of the people you encounter will at least tolerate your humor and, in many instances, enjoy it. As one CEO told me, "I tend to be stiff and sober, but I do appreciate others' humor." So, take the risk. Just keep telling yourself that people are probably smiling on the inside.

4. *Plan for spontaneity.* Store up some anecdotes that relate to situations you are likely to encounter.

All business humor isn't off the cuff. For instance, after a fairly impressive introduction, Robert W. Galvin, chairman of the Executive Committee of Motorola, Inc. (and son of the founder), would say, "I want to thank our host for omitting from the reasons for my rapid rise the most important detail of all, the fact that my dad owns the joint." He used virtually the same quip to open a few of his public speeches—and it always got a laugh.

You can't always rely on a quick wit. That's why many businesspeople and politicians have joke writers create a backlog of seemingly spontaneous stories that they can insert into conversations when necessary. "I have fall-back stories," one CEO told me. "That way, if some faux pas is made, I can salvage the situation."

5. *If you can't bring yourself to initiate being humorous, at least look for, recognize, and reward others' attempts at levity.* You'll reduce tension, ease communication difficulties, show your humanness, and make work more fun.

6. *But don't go overboard.* Anything good taken to extremes becomes bad. Your sense of humor will work against you (and as you feared, prevent you from being taken seriously) if you overuse it.

16

Ask Favors. Form Bonds.

"The first thing I do when I arrive for an appointment is ask for a cup of coffee," said Mike Hirshorn. Recruited while in his early thirties to be president of Cochlear AG/Australia, he has since been named one of the twelve outstanding business leaders in Australia.

"I'm careful not to do this in a way that makes anyone feel awkward for not offering me a cup first," he continued. "But I do ask and I ask for two reasons. One, I would like a cup of coffee, and two, I want to ask them to do me a favor. If I have to wait to meet with an individual, I will ask if I can use the boardroom to make some phone calls. I'll ask to borrow a pen and paper. I'll ask a secretary to check my flight schedule. I'll use any excuse. But I will always ask a favor."

Why? For the same reason generations of women have engaged in the stereotypical action of dropping a handkerchief so a man will pick it up. It makes the person doing the favor feel valued, important, and flattered (or for that man retrieving the handkerchief—chivalrous and gentlemanly). It also gives the person asking the favor an opportunity to repay it—and start a relationship with the person to whom he or she is now indebted.

Although our natural inclination is to get closer to others by doing favors *for* them, that rarely produces the effect we desire or intend. When we do people favors, we create obligations. They now owe us, and their being indebted to us makes them feel uncomfortable in our presence rather than receptive to us. Doing favors, creating obligations, and then "calling in our markers" may have worked in *The Godfather*, but it is not an effective way to form bonds and develop business relationships.

We also make a mistake by being too nicey-nice and doing, doing, doing for others—even when our well-meaning intent is to bond. We end up looking too eager to please. Or we twist ourselves into a pretzel to give people what they want, only to discover for the umpteenth time that the people to whom we are kindest are the ones who turn around and abuse us the most.

Doing favors is a form of rescuing, and it does not build bonds. It creates resentments. We've all seen it happen. We lend people money and they seem angry at us when they have to pay it back. Or they don't pay us back and avoid us. Either way we lose.

Although I'm not saying you shouldn't do favors for others at all, at least initially you are better off asking for favors and being the one in debt. (You can always pay back what you "owe" by doing for them what you planned to do anyway.) People prefer to "do for," rather than to be "done for." Or as the late Malcolm Forbes put it, "It's being asked that pleases most."

I first noticed the positive effect of asking favors when I was visiting one of the top people I interviewed for this book. Out of the blue, he asked me to help him rearrange some office furniture. My initial reaction was to think, "Do it yourself." But I almost immediately changed my tune. "He must really value my opinion," I thought and was soon hard at work, eagerly trying to do a good job so I could prove that his confidence in me was well placed. Although that executive claimed he did not ask the favor in order to have that effect on me, once I was aware of the behavior (and its outcome), I started to watch other top people to see if they did it, too. They do.

SUCCESSFUL PEOPLE ASK FOR FAVORS

Asking for favors helps top people bond with and show that they value the person asked. Their requests are rarely a "big deal" or for something people must go out of their way to accomplish. But in the asking, a compliment is paid and others are reassured of their worth.

1. *Asking for favors makes the person asked feel important and included.* "I need your help to make this project a success," Ryal Poppa, chairman, president, and CEO of Storage Technology Corporation, said to his management team at a meeting I attended. Right before my eyes "the" project became "their" project, one which they were more willing than ever to support because Poppa had let them know that their contribution to it was vital and would be appreciated. Good managers ask favors for precisely that reason.

2. *Asking a favor says "I value your opinion," and "our relationship matters to me. I want us to continue working together."* It's now second nature for me to ask favors. For instance, whenever I complete an assignment for someone, I say, "Would you write a brief note telling me what you thought about my advice? Your feedback would be very helpful to me." My clients hear that I too have needs and appreciate their input as much as they needed mine. My request also strengthens the bond we formed while I was working for them.

3. *Asking favors not only makes the person asked feel valuable and effective but also can have a powerful impact on the people who see you ask.* One well-known CEO and I were having lunch when we happened to see an ex-company president I'll call Joe and another man together at a table on the other side of the restaurant. We both knew that Joe's company, because of bad business decisions and a poor economy, had recently failed and he had filed for bankruptcy. We had heard that he was trying—thus far in vain—to get funding to start a new venture. The CEO I was lunching with recognized the "other man" as a prospective financier.

The CEO went over to their table and said, "Joe, what a pleasant surprise. I've been trying to call your office. May I join you for a drink?" He had "asked a favor" that made Joe feel (and look) important—as if it would be an honor to join his table.

Then the CEO asked another favor. This time, addressing the financier, he said, "Do you mind if I get Joe's opinion on some financial questions?" and proceeded to discuss some seemingly important numbers with Joe. There could be no doubt in the mind of anyone watching that the CEO valued Joe's input. His asking favors had not only complimented Joe but also empowered him as well. The financier could not help but hold Joe in higher esteem.

As you can see, asking for favors does not mean borrowing money or asking your boss to give your son-in-law a job. The nature of the favors you seek will vary from situation to situation and from relationship to relationship. Occasionally favor exchanges can turn into complex systems of debits and credits.

"Bill" and "Craig" were due to drive together to an industry social gathering. Craig had agreed to pick up Bill at seven in the evening, but at six-thirty, Bill called Craig and asked him to come at seven-thirty instead. Although Craig was actually ready to go, he said, "Fine. That will give me an excuse for my own tardiness." By doing Bill a favor but making it sound as if Bill were doing him a favor, Craig minimized Bill's feeling of obligation. He no longer "owed" Craig. Then, Craig purposely did not pick Bill up until seven-forty-five. His tardiness absolved Bill of any responsibility for the delay. In fact, Craig asked Bill for another favor—to excuse him for being late.

Asking favors can take the form of seeking someone's advice. I've yet to meet anyone who doesn't love giving his opinion or won't feel flattered by your request. A good rule of thumb is this: If you would be annoyed if someone asked the same favor of you, then the favor you are about to ask probably is out of line.

To ask a favor effectively:

1. Operate from a desire to make someone feel needed.
2. Smile.
3. Say something like, "Could I get your help with . . ." or "You've always been good at . . . , would you. . . ."
4. Say thank you.
5. Compliment the giver.

Asking favors works. It's not "kissing up." It is human, a little humble, a way to say "you are necessary, valuable, and important," and a most sincere form of flattery.

17

Ask Questions—
The Answers Help You Manage

"Before I turned a screw on this company, I spent thirteen weeks asking prospective customers what they wanted from a vendor. I visited thirty-six individuals and filled nine yellow ledger pads with the things I learned about products, service, delivery, and introducing a new company. My questioning created the foundation for Contel Customer Support."

—DAVID FANNING
President, GTE Customer Network

TOP PEOPLE ASK QUESTIONS

Successful people do not necessarily have more answers than anyone else. They do ask more questions. As they climb higher and higher up the corporate ladder, top people become farther and farther removed from "the action." By asking questions they stay in touch with the people they manage and on top of the problems they are called upon to solve.

Most leaders are experts at asking questions. However, asking questions is vitally important at every level of the business world. You could almost make it to the top with no other ability but the ability to ask questions effectively—and you literally cannot lead without it.

> "Even when I have my own ideas about a situation, I ask people 'What do *you* see here?' or 'What would *you* do here?' or 'How would *you* do it?' instead of telling them what I think they should do."
>
> —JEFF SMULYAN
> *Owner, the Seattle Mariners*

1. *Questioning is an essential tool for good management.* It takes less time and effort to tell your subordinates how to solve a problem than to ask for their point of view. If they respect your judgment (or fear the consequences of disagreeing with you), they will probably do as you say. However, you boost morale and insure that the problem will be attacked more efficiently, effectively, and enthusiastically by allowing the people who will be executing your ideas to be involved in the problem-solving and decision-making process. Asking questions enables you to do that. It is a basic people skill.

2. *Questions create human connections.* Rather than appearing solely self-centered, by asking questions you give other people their "two minutes in the spotlight." As a result, they view you in a more favorable light and feel closer to you.

With such questions as "How's your cold—any better?", "Did you run into much traffic on your way in?" or "Where did you find that chair? I've been looking all over for one like it," you communicate your interest in others as people, building a foundation for person-to-person business relationships. In addition, as explained in the previous chapter, asking for advice is a classic form of asking for a favor. It flatters people, affirms them, and makes them feel important.

"As I see it, my job is to be a facilitator—to clear the garbage out of the way so my people can do *their* jobs. I don't claim to have all the smarts. I know I need as much information as possible from the people doing the job. I get it by asking questions."

—ALVAR GREEN
Chairman, president, and CEO, Autodesk, Inc.

3. *Asking questions keeps you from being a know-it-all (and getting tripped up by what you really don't know).* Even if you think you do know it all, you are wise to ask questions. Sometimes your questions will generate answers you'd prefer not to hear. But it's better to hear something you dislike and deal with it than to hold on to your own cherished (or naive) notions and have the situation you did not ask about blow up in your face.

4. *Questions buy time.* Questions can give you the time to decide on your own response or a course of action. You can also postpone or avoid confrontations or attacks on your character. Questioning is particularly effective when you are caught off guard or being criticized. Simply ask, "What do you mean?" Be sure to use an even tone of voice and not a defensive or challenging one.

"Recently, I was picked up at the airport by one of my employees and tried to get a status report on business in his city. I asked, 'How are things?' and he assured me that everything was 'fine.' But I kept probing and eventually found out that his initial 'no problem' was an understatement, to say the least. In fact, we were about to lose three of our largest accounts! It took twenty minutes of directed questions to discover the truth, but it was worth it because once I knew about the problem, I was able to do something about it."

—ALEX J. MANDL
Chairman and CEO, Sea Land Service, Inc.

5. *By asking questions, you can steer conversations in the direction you want them to go—the one that tells you what you need to know.* To get the most from business conversations, decide where you're going to start and where you want to go— then let questions take you there. Don't hesitate to ask questions from notes or write down the answers. However, you need not have a previously prepared list of questions, and you don't have to stay glued to a particular line of questioning. Let the interchange take on a life of its own. But, as needed, direct or redirect the conversation with questions.

You can ask questions to start, to maintain, and subsequently to end conversations. For instance, whether I have called the meeting or someone else has, one of my favorite openings is to look the other person in the eye, smile, and with an easy, inquisitive tone of voice, ask, "Would you like to start?" I almost always close by saying "Have we covered everything?" or "Is there anything you'd like to add before we wrap this up?"

6. *And when should you stop asking questions? When you have the information you want or need.* One of the most effective techniques for selling products and negotiating contracts involves asking questions to learn someone else's position before revealing yours. In fact, sales training programs teach their students to get customers to do at least 70 percent of the talking and to talk no more than 30 percent of the time themselves. A customer reveals the best way to sell to him when you ask:

- What do you want to achieve?
- What do you want to maintain?
- What do you want to avoid?
- Who makes the decisions?
- How do they make decisions?
- When will they make decisions?
- Do they have the money to pay?
- What do you need to know from me?

- What do you need to know to make the decision to go with us?
- What is your decision?

7. *Asking questions is also the answer to the problem of making small talk, which so many of us dislike.* It helps you break the ice and get conversations going without running the risk of talking too much yourself. The next time you are at a conference, convention, or business-related social function, after your usual "How do you do?" ask:

- "What brings you to this party?"
- "How do you happen to know the hosts?"
- "I understand you're in (occupation). What do you think about (issue)?"
- "You said you're with XYZ company? What is the main thrust of the company now?"

Just pick a topic and attach a "who, what, when, where, or how" to it. You'll discover that you have something in common (and something to talk about) with almost anyone you meet.

You gain and hold someone's attention better with a question than with a statement. And you feel less pressure to perform. The situation becomes less intimidating because you no longer need to come up with something brilliant or totally original to say. Just ask a question. You'll relax and in turn relax others.

8. *Questions get results—tactfully.* I was riding the pastures with a farmer friend in his pickup truck when we saw two people walking their dogs—and trespassing on his land. Because there were some fifty newborn calves in the pasture with their mothers that day and the farmer did not want the dogs to chase the calves, cause a stampede, and separate the calves from their mothers, he needed to get the dogs and their owners off his property.

We drove up to the trespassers and my friend asked, "Did you know this is private property?" They did. "Well, then, did you know that we shoot dogs that get close to the calves?" was his next question.

"We'll leave right away," was the dog walkers' reply.

The farmer smiled, thanked them, and closed the conversation with, "Nice day for a walk."

Even though he rightfully could have ordered the people to leave his land, the farmer achieved his goal efficiently, effectively, and without a conflict or confrontation through the questions he asked. The same practice has a similar effect up and down the corporate ladder and throughout the business world.

9. *And of course, if you ask questions, you might actually learn something new.* While on assignment in San Diego, I overheard one businessman saying to another, "I couldn't figure out what you wanted me to say or if you wanted me to wonder about what you said. I wasn't exactly sure how I should take it. If I didn't hear you correctly, then I could have misinterpreted the second thing you said because I had misunderstood the first statement you made." The second businessman looked at his colleague quizzically and said, "Well, why didn't you just ask me what I meant?"

The first businessman did not ask because, like so many of us, he was concerned about *appearing* uninformed when his real concern should have been actually *being* uninformed. Choosing not to inquire for fear of looking dumb is one of the dumbest things you can do. If you don't know, ask. You'll avoid mutual mystification. You'll get the answers you need to solve immediate problems and be more well informed in the future as well.

And remember—subordinates emulate the boss. By demonstrating that asking questions is acceptable and not a sign of weakness or stupidity, you create a climate where others will feel free to ask questions themselves.

HOW TO ASK QUESTIONS EFFECTIVELY

1. *Give yourself permission to inquire.* Don't wait for an invitation. By the time someone asks "Any questions?" you may have lost your thought—and the opportunity to learn something new. Unless you are specifically requested to hold your questions (until the end of a lecture, for instance), ask a question if you need an answer. If you're curious, inquire. If you want to come away from a meeting with the information you need to do your job well, be prepared to ask questions, start posing them early on, and continue asking throughout.

2. *Ask in a way that truly invites a response.* If you pose your questions in a manner that is (or can be misconstrued as) threatening, punitive, retaliatory, or interrogating, you'll put people on the defensive, shut down communication, and get very few useful answers. Control your voice and your attitude. An even tone, a smile, and an air of open-minded acceptance convey genuine interest and get the best results. The most effective voice for almost any situation, and particularly when you run the risk of becoming overly excited or emotional, is the same one you use when you say, "Would you please pass the salt?"

3. *Ask more than one question.* One inquiry may hardly scratch the surface. To learn, bond, build rapport, and keep conversations flowing, ask a question, volunteer some information of your own, then ask additional questions. It is also beneficial to encourage others to say more with comments such as:

- "Hmm, that's intriguing, tell me more."
- "Keep talking. You're giving me some excellent information."
- "You are doing a great job explaining this. I appreciate it. Please continue."

4. *Use common sense and good judgment.* Don't question at random, jumping from topic to topic with no apparent rhyme or reason. Listen. Tailor your next question to what you have heard and explain any rapid changes of direction you take. Let the other person know that their remark triggered a new line of thought and raised a question that seemed to have no direct connection to what preceded it.

Question in good taste. Know what not to ask and be sensitive to cultural, racial, ethnic, regional, or gender differences that might make a question that would not offend you seem offensive to others. If you inadvertently "hit a nerve" or ask a question that seems to turn someone three shades of pale, stop right then, ask "Did I ask something inappropriate?" and apologize.

5. *Don't ask trick questions or wage probing attacks.* "Why on earth did you do that?" "What made you think I'd go for this idea?" "Don't you agree that my idea is better?" "Weren't you paying attention?" These are examples of questions that are impossible for people to answer without "incriminating" themselves or getting into an argument with you. They are ineffective and generally uncalled for. So are questions that have no answers, questions to which you already know the answers (designed to trap people in lies), and questions that search for vulnerabilities or attempt to expose others as irresponsible, negligent, stupid, or incompetent. Don't ask them. If people discover that you "ask to attack," they will begin to avoid you. So stick to real questions, specific questions, and questions that accomplish positive outcomes.

If someone uses questions to trap or attack *you*, question them to deflect the attack. With a relaxed facial expression and calm, even tone of voice, ask "What do you mean?", "Could you explain what you're getting at?" or "Would you mind rephrasing your question? I'm not sure I understand what you're asking." Adding "I'm sorry, I still don't understand what you mean" and maintaining the same relaxed facial expression and tone, repeat your questions until the other person stops interrogating or challenging you and starts communicating with you more openly.

6. *Prepare questions in advance.* Although you don't have to carry a double-spaced, typed list of twenty questions with you at all times and whip it out to "probe" at appropriate intervals, it does help to have at least a few preplanned questions to carry you through any occasion. Whether you are selling or hearing a sales pitch, negotiating a contract or dealing with the media, you'll be better equipped to handle the situation if you've given some advance thought to questions you might ask. Here are a few standard ones that you can fall back on almost anytime with almost anyone.

- "Can you tell me more?"
- "How do you feel about (something you just told them, they just told you or you both just witnessed)?"
- "What problems have you encountered in . . .?"
- "What are your competitors doing in . . .?"
- "What are the customers complaints about . . .?"
- "What do you think about . . .?"

7. *Listen—to what is being said (and what isn't).* What you hear (and what you don't) often raises additional questions in your mind. Asking those questions is an integral part of being a good listener. Your probing lets others know you are paying attention to them and encourages them to say more. Using their input when making a decision, for instance, or dealing with a problem they brought to your attention during a subsequent conversation, or simply mentioning something they shared with you increases their sense of contribution and their respect for you.

8. *If you don't want to hear the answer and especially if you don't want to do anything about what you hear—don't ask the question.* In the best of all possible worlds, the answers to every question you ask would please you, confirm your competence, and reassure you that everything around you was running smoothly. In the real world, that is not always the case. On the plus side, if you are alerted to "bad news" before it happens or as soon as possible after the fact, you can make contingency plans to deal with it or quickly embark upon damage control. However, sometimes:

- There is nothing you *can* do—about someone's disgruntled feelings, for example, or about giving people pay raises during a period of cutbacks and layoffs.
- You're too swamped with other details to do anything about lower priority problems, such as the quality of food in the company cafeteria or the rivalry building between your advertising and public relations departments.
- New or additional information is the last thing you need. After ordering that new telephone system, it does not help to hear about a better system that has just become available.
- While putting together your annual report, there comes a time when receiving one more suggestion about one more human interest angle to include is counterproductive.

Under these and similar circumstances, it really is wiser *not* to ask questions.

QUESTIONING IS A TWO-WAY STREET

Obviously, during any given business day, you will not only be in a position to ask questions but also be called upon to answer them. How you respond to other people's inquiries affects the initial impression you make, your rapport with the person asking the question, and your ability to maintain some semblance of control over yourself and the situation. There are several options available to you. They are:

- Answer the question honestly and straightforwardly. Do not select this option if using it would violate someone's confidentiality. It is not necessary or appropriate to tell anyone that Joe used to have a drinking problem or that your assistant has been less outgoing since she miscarried—even if you are asked about that individual's past or present behavior.

- Buy time or obtain additional information by asking a clarifying question: "Are you asking for a general financial picture or specific figures?" or "Could you give me an idea about what sort of information you're looking for?"
- Use a story to illustrate your answer.
- Use humor to lighten the impact of the question or the answer.
- Admit when you've been stumped. Don't hesitate to say, "I don't know the answer for that. I'll look into it and get back to you." Realize that your credibility will be damaged if you don't follow through on that commitment. An alternative might be to refer the person asking the question to someone who can answer his question or suggest that he do a little digging and then let you know what he comes up with.
- Answer and then ask for feedback or encourage further discussion. When I interviewed Fritz Maytag, president and brewmaster of Anchor Brewing Company, he followed up most of his responses by asking "Did that answer your question?" and more often "What do you think?" or "Don't they?" By doing so, he used the interview to obtain information as well as dispense it.

Asking questions, answering them, then probing a little deeper and uncovering a little more is the essence of communication. It is how you learn what you need to know and build the rapport you need to have in order to manage and lead effectively. It is also a tool for self-management. In the quiet of your home or office, review your efforts and improve upon them by asking yourself: "Did I do a good job? What could I have done better? What will I do next time?" Asking and answering such questions helps you learn, grow, and succeed in business and in life.

III

MOVE AHEAD—THE ART OF SELF-REALIZATION

18

The Philosophy of Chiefs

As explained back in chapter 1, successful people:

- stand out to get in;
- fit in to get ahead;
- and then stand out and fit in at the same time to get to the top.

They distinguish themselves and demonstrate their leadership ability by doing what others don't—without going to extremes.

CHIEFS ADOPT A PHILOSOPHY OF OPTIMISM

Day in and day out top people present their best selves to the world and bring out the best in others. How do they accomplish that feat? By adopting a *philosophy of optimism* and a positive "most-things-are-possible" attitude.

Ernie Howell, retired president of St. Regis/WPM, epitomizes that philosophy ("despite my Rice University engineering background," he laughs). Although he has lived and worked in or visited enough foreign countries to be blasé about world travel, when I asked him, "What's the best trip you've ever taken?" he replied, without a moment's hesitation, "The next one." On another occasion, when he was preparing to undergo surgery and treatment for a medical problem, I asked him how long it would take to recover. His response was, "For most people, six weeks, for me, two." Top people consistently choose to display and maintain that same sort of optimism.

> "Every day I wake up thinking that something wonderful is going to happen to me. Even when it doesn't—which is often—I think it will happen the next day."
> —JIM RUPP
> *Attorney*

People with a philosophy of optimism believe in themselves and their abilities. They are sure of and in charge of their goals, their thoughts, their behavior, and how they affect others. They select and control their outlook. Just as athletes condition their bodies for competition, people with a philosophy of optimism mentally condition themselves for success.

> "Am I really different? Maybe not, but I sure say and feel that I am."
> —LARRY COLIN
> *President, Colin Service Systems, Inc.*

> "You can manage problems but you can't prevent them. The same holds true for your thoughts. You have to manage them and not avoid them. . . . I plant thoughts in my mind that include reasonable hope and reasonable predictions of positive outcomes. I presume that things will turn out favorably if certain favorable things take place."
> —RALPH ABLON
> *Chairman, Ogden Corporation*

Optimistic people expect to succeed. First they dream, then they plan, then they execute their plans. But they would not have found the impetus to go after their dreams (or dream them) if they had not already suspected that they would be successful. As David Chamberlain, president, and CEO, of Shaklee Corporation, put it, "The reason these top people get to be CEOs is because they want to be CEOs and they tell themselves they *can* be CEOs."

> "Even when I was financially strapped, I didn't feel it. Even when I was absolutely broke, I knew I would make it. Sometimes people set their sights too low and then become trapped by their own frame of reference. I've learned that you have to look for your North Star, but the minute you reach it, you need to scrap that dream and pick a new one to set your spirit free again. You can't continue to hold on to dreams already achieved—it will oxidize your brain."
>
> —GLENN R. JONES
> *CEO, Jones Intercable, Inc.*

Because they believe "I can make this happen and I'm going to figure out how to do it," people with a philosophy of optimism usually do succeed.

Of course, a good attitude doesn't *guarantee* success, but it still beats a bad attitude. In some situations, pessimists will be proven right, but optimists will always have a better time. It is also more fun and more inspiring to be around them. Their philosophy has a positive effect on their family, friends, employees, competitors, and everyone else in their private and professional lives. In fact, one of the most compelling reasons to adopt a philosophy of optimism is for its impact on others.

As I've said, people draw conclusions about you based on what they see. And whether or not you are consciously aware of it, your philosophy is visible to others at all times. It is evident everywhere—in person, on paper, during the speeches you give, while you are hiring, firing, reprimanding, running a meeting, walking down the hallway, and on and on. At different times with different people, it can work for you or against you, but it is always there.

An effective philosophy is measured by relationships built or lost. One secret of success in dealing with others is to make sure that your attitude is upbeat.

Like changing the channels and volume on your television set with a remote-control device, when you control your outlook and beliefs about yourself, others, your work, and life in general you generate an optimistic attitude and present yourself as you'd prefer to be perceived. According to the chiefs I've interviewed, it is vitally important to do that.

> "If you don't believe in yourself, you'd better know that no one else will. You haven't got a hope in hell."
> —GORDON PARKER
> *Chairman, president, and CEO,*
> *Newmont Mining Corporation*

SUCCESS STARTS WITH (AND BUILDS) CONFIDENCE

> "Editorial writing is pretty cheeky. You sit down, look at the world, and go tell the experts what they are doing wrong. You don't have to be right all the time. You do need to think about what you are doing, its impact, meaning, justification. And you need the self-confidence to do it."
> —ROBERT BARTLEY
> The Wall Street Journal

It takes self-confidence to do any job. It takes even more self-confidence to do what others don't—and make it to the top. All chiefs are self-confident but not necessarily at all times or under all circumstances.

"The first thing I had to do this morning was kick off a United Way breakfast. I perspire more in that kind of situation than if I were talking to ten thousand people. These things aren't as organized as I'd like. The cast of characters involved changes and I can't prepare. People are judging you as if this is all you have to do all day. It's not easy for me. It's easier with experience, but still not easy."

—DAVE CARPENTER
Chairman, president, and CEO,
Transamerica Occidental Life Insurance

Someone who could breeze through that United Way breakfast might sweat bullets while writing a paper for publication or anxiously toss and turn the entire night before appearing on a television talk show. We all have self-confidence in some situations—situations we are familiar with and where we have experienced some success. Top people simply have self-confidence (or at least the appearance of it) in more situations than less successful individuals.

Still, the person without self-doubt is living in a dream world. Self-confidence is really a feeling of adequacy. You have to feel adequate and comfortable with yourself to make it to the top. But no one at the top feels adequate in every situation or is certain that he is correct all of the time. Few acts are undertaken with *complete* certainty, and the person who appears always to be sure of everything is generally faking it. We don't trust and are reluctant to be led by people who seem *too* sure of themselves.

Top people simply have *enough* confidence to take the risks they need to take to succeed. They actually feel certain more frequently than most of us, and because they are at the helm, they understand the need to appear sure of themselves when they walk into a room, shake hands, and begin to speak.

Top people are comfortable with themselves. They also know how to look comfortable while doing uncomfortable things. They are neither overly self-assured nor fearful of being exposed to scrutiny because they *know what they can do and are able to deal with their fears.*

> "I access back to something I accomplished that I thought was beyond my reach, and it gives me a vitamin shot of confidence. Then I talk out loud to myself about my fears. I'll have an imaginary conversation, think about the worst, and tell myself how to handle it. I almost always conclude, 'Hey, I can do this.' "
>
> —**BOB BERKOWITZ**
> *Host, "Real Personal," CNBC*

Some top people seem to have been born confident. They say they have felt sure of themselves for as long as they can remember. Others trace their powerful belief in their own abilities to a specific event or time in their life. For instance, during high school, Bill Daniels, chairman of Daniels Communications, "whipped the town bully" in a dispute about a girl. "I've never lacked confidence since," he said. Many chiefs developed self-confidence by prospering in areas where their peers floundered—academics, sports, dating, and so on.

Someone who has had more than one success is apt to be self-confident. Three seems to be the magic number. The first success is sometimes dismissed as luck. The second could be "lightning striking twice." But the third success in the same area is generally accepted as resulting from your actions and feeds your confidence. Repeated successes teach you not to be afraid to try, and that in turn leads to more success—and more self-confidence. As Larry Colin, president of Colin Service Systems, Inc., put it, "Once you have enough success, it goes directly to your posture and then to your attitude."

At a critical point in his career, Tom Freston, president and CEO of MTV Networks, took a year off and traveled around the world. He said, "I found my way, improvised, survived. I felt more confident when I returned. You gain confidence through an experience like that. You realize you're as good as anybody else—you just lacked confidence before. Confidence is just being willing to try things."

Although position and possessions do not necessarily increase confidence, "money in the bank" often will. It gives you options and choices. One chief I interviewed told me, "I carry a thousand-dollar bill at all times. It's tucked in my wallet—and in my psyche. I know I can buy almost anything I see if I want to. I seldom do. Just knowing I can is sufficient."

Money in the bank keeps you from feeling stuck or powerless. You are more willing to take risks when you know that no matter what happens you won't be destitute.

> "If you don't have money, you feel you don't have anything to back you up. When I started my career, I always kept one month's salary in the bank so I could say, 'I quit.' I didn't have to put up with stuff I didn't want to deal with. That financial security boosted my ego. Without it, I wouldn't have had the confidence to go out and do the other things I needed to do."
>
> —ERNIE HOWELL
> *Retired president, St. Regis/WPM*

Money in the bank, promotions, awards, compliments, corner offices, and other tangible signs of your competence and success *boost* self-confidence. However, to feel truly sure of yourself (and make it to the top) your sense of adequacy and self-worth must come from within. If it does not, you will relentlessly collect "trophies" to prove your own worth and compensate for your insecurities. And you won't fool anybody for long. A highly polished surface will get you only so far.

As a consultant, I don't *give* my clients confidence, I help them build it from the inside out by pointing out and reminding them of their past successes as well as recommending new behaviors that can improve their performance in the future. As their ability to control their actions and how they affect others increases, their self-confidence does too.

How to Increase Your Self-Confidence

1. *Relax and look back.* Sit down, take out a ledger, and list your successes. Include minor as well as major accomplishments and situations you handled well if not perfectly (or as well as you could handle them now). Go back as far as grade school if you'd like, and try not to miss anything you have done that you initially doubted you could do. Hang on to your list. Add to it periodically and reread it when you're feeling insecure. Reminding yourself of your past successes is an effective way to restore your self-confidence.

2. *Make sure you're in a job you enjoy and be extremely competent in that job.* When you derive satisfaction from your job, you are likely to do it well. You give it your all while you're in it and are motivated to become even more competent at it. Competence breeds confidence. As long as you're good in your chosen field, you won't feel a pressing need to be good at everything—which, of course, is impossible.

To be competent and confident, you must also believe in the work you do. If you don't, think about changing jobs or careers. You may be in the wrong field or position. Many of us find ourselves in that situation temporarily. If we stay in it despite our reservations, it catches up with us. One day we wake up, look in the bathroom mirror, and dislike the person we see. It's your choice. Yes, it takes guts to make a career change. But if you take the risk and make a move to the occupation of your choice, the dissatisfaction that is preventing you from being as competent and confident as you can be will disappear and your chances for success will improve dramatically.

3. *Pat yourself on the back.* Even small steps toward a goal deserve recognition. And you don't have to go "fishing" for compliments from others in order to get the "atta boys" you've earned. Look at each new accomplishment and say, "I did that and I did it well." You feel more capable, adequate, and comfortable with yourself when you approve of yourself and tell yourself that you've done a good job.

4. Work on boosting others' confidence. Spread compliments around. They work wonders.

> "People work for love and money and seldom get enough of either. Flattery, even false flattery, feels good. It's amazing how little people get complimented. Explain how valuable they are and do it in writing on a constant basis. Before they go home on Friday, tell them what they did right last week. Tell your spouse she or he is good every day. No one ever gets enough praise."
>
> —JACK FALVEY
> *President, Intermark*

Tell people you believe in them. Recognize the possibility that they might be right and you might be wrong. Allow them to make mistakes and encourage them to make decisions. Your faith in them helps them maintain their confidence when their decisions end up as mistakes.

What do you get in return? Positive, productive working relationships, the knowledge that they were the result of your actions, and more confidence in your ability to manage, lead, and relate to others.

5. Accept and understand occasional self-doubt. But don't succumb to it. Face small fears and everyday doubts head on and tackle them one by one. Stop worrying so much. Accept yourself and your role and repeat to yourself, "I am what I am and that's okay." Remind yourself that you have made mistakes, recovered from them, and likely will make mistakes again. To make it to the top, you simply must corral self-doubt and whip it into shape with positive self-talk.

Top people have an optimistic attitude about themselves and maintain it with positive self-talk. The comments I've *never* heard from top people (but do hear from people who have not made it) include:

- "My job isn't turning out as I thought it would. I really don't like it, but I can't do anything about it."
- "I'm exhausted. I can't find the energy to get everything done, and I'm so far behind that I'll never catch up."
- "Other people get all the breaks. I'm never in the right place at the right time."
- "Things would be different if I were. . . ." (Choose one or more: older, younger, smarter, better looking, white, black, female, male, in a larger company, in a smaller company, in a different industry, in a different city, had gone to a better school.)
- "I'm not any good at _____." (Fill in the blank.)

Just because top people don't say these things does not mean that they never feel downhearted or that their problems are nonexistent. However, they have learned to *control the self-judging thoughts they express to others and repeat to themselves.* As a result, they are able to maintain the positive outlook they need to lead effectively and succeed in business.

> "All our lives and at all times we have private discussions going on inside our heads. We write letters to ourselves. Make speeches to ourselves. And we become what we tell ourselves. Believing you can get self-esteem from someone else is a trap. There are no external solutions to internal problems."
>
> —RALPH ABLON
> *Chairman, Ogden Corporation*

> "It all comes down to your own self-belief. If you believe you're okay, one day you'll wake up and find you truly are."
>
> —JEFF SMULYAN
> *Owner, the Seattle Mariners*

"Don't say, 'I can't, I won't.' You must say, 'I can, I will.' "

—RYAL POPPA
Chairman, president, and CEO
Storage Technology Corporation

Success comes to people who believe they will be successful. They make it because they think they can and act accordingly.

Conversely, members of the SNP (Society of Negative People) frequently fail. They fill their heads with so many pessimistic thoughts and gloomy forecasts that they literally talk themselves into failure.

One of my clients was telling me about a situation he believed he had handled poorly and concluded his tale of woe by saying, "But then, I'm a real jerk anyway."

I sat there a moment and then, with a straight face and even tone of voice, said, "Oh, I see, you're a real jerk. . . ."

Upon hearing his words directed back at him like that, an alarmed expression appeared on my client's face. He said, "You know, I don't like the sound of that." Yet he had been saying it to himself for years, and even though he was not a jerk, thanks to his negative opinion of himself, he gave himself permission to act as if he were one.

When you think negatively, your negative thoughts are translated into behavior without you even realizing it. Others hear your ruminations. They observe your lethargic, downtrodden appearance. They sense your negative feelings about yourself and your lack of confidence in your abilities. And they have no more faith in you than you have in yourself.

"I don't discriminate against women or minorities. I do, however, suspect anyone who is defensive about themselves. It's harder to accept people who don't accept themselves."

—CURT CARTER
Chairman, Mission Bay Investments, Inc.

Your perception of yourself influences everything you do or don't do, attempt or avoid, welcome or fear, and it makes an enormous difference in the way others perceive you. That is why it is so important to manage the mental images that constantly run through your mind and your self-talk—the things you tell yourself about who you are, your circumstances, and your potential to succeed. In a world where so many things are beyond your control, your attitude toward yourself is something you can control—and must if you want to make it to the top and stay there.

ASSIGN YOUR MIND THE PHILOSOPHY YOU WANT

"It took me to old age to discover that the more I worry, the more the things I worried about happened."

—YAP LIM SEN
Managing director, IGB Corporation Berhad

In your mind's eye, reality is whatever you think it is. If you think you are dumb, timid, inarticulate, or a real jerk, your psyche accepts your evaluation, and the next time you encounter a situation that requires smarts, courage, verbal expressiveness, or compassion, it remembers what you told it. It tells *you* that you can't handle the situation, undermining your confidence and hampering your ability to choose and follow the best possible course of action.

Fortunately, the same process works in reverse. By planting positive images in your mind and repeating positive thoughts to yourself, you can reprogram your psyche to respond favorably to situations that once baffled or defeated you.

Negative thinking is a mental habit and, like any habit, it won't be easy to break. It will take time and effort to clear away the negative muck and replace it with a positive philosophy. But the result is worth the time and energy you'll invest. Your entire outlook improves when you tell your psyche what you want it to tell you. Like top people, you'll succeed where others don't because you'll hear optimistic, productive, solution-oriented self-talk when you think, review, rehash, critique, and anticipate.

If other people talked to us as we talk to ourselves, we'd never talk to them again! Keep that in mind the next time you catch yourself using negative self-talk. Then shut out that self-talk immediately. *Stop putting yourself down* out loud and inside your head.

1. *Assign your mind a positive attitude instead.* While one of the chiefs I interviewed was playing nine holes of golf alone, I rode around in a golf cart with him and heard him say to himself: "Keep that left knee steady"; "I'm going to hit the next shot farther to the right"; "Slug this one"; "A ten iron, that's plenty, choke it down a little"; "Play it low into the wind, hit it hard."

He was assigning his mind—mentally preparing himself—for the task at hand. From time to time he also literally addressed the ball. "Come on down, come on down," he'd say. Or "Don't go into the sand." When I seemed amused by that practice, he shrugged and said, "Sometimes it listens."

Sometimes it didn't. And as much as that chief talked himself into it, he did not hit perfect shots every time. But he got better results from his positive preparation than he would have with no preparation or negative preparation. (For instance, if he'd said, "You klutz, couldn't you do better than that?"; "What's the matter with you? How could you miss that shot?"; "The way you're playing today, you might as well pack it in"; "You'll never get out of this sand trap.")

None of us gets everything he is seeking. However, since we can get a good percentage of what we are striving for, it pays to strive for more. Optimists know that, which is why they generally end up with more than people who take a pessimistic approach.

"I have a positive attitude toward work even if things go poorly. I think, 'Next time I'll do it better.' Sometimes it's two steps forward and three steps back, but none of us is infallible, so I just pick up and remain focused."

—ROSE MARIE BRAVO
President, I. Magnin, Inc.

2. *Choose your perspective.* When you *don't* succeed, you can:

- say you're a failure;
- think about all the things you should have done;
- tell yourself that you might as well give up because you clearly don't have what it takes to make it.

Or you can:

- say you've learned something you didn't know before;
- think about how you will use that information in the future;
- tell yourself that now that you know what not to do next time, you are closer than ever to achieving your goal.

It's up to you. Attitudes are chosen. You can choose the one you want.

3. *Make a commitment to control your self-talk and therefore your life. Belief determines behavior.* Replace beliefs that don't work for you with ones that do. Say "when I succeed" instead of "if"; "I will" or "I'll try" instead of "I can't"; "I'll get it right next time," instead of "I won't make the same mistake." These subtle shifts can create a complete attitudinal turnaround. With your old pessimistic outlook, you tried to avoid failure and frequently chose not to take the risks that could have brought you success. With your new philosophy of optimism (and positive self-talk) you strive for success and more often get it.

4. *Make mental movies using affirmative self-talk as a life script. Then live it.* Instead of agonizing over where you'll be if your plans fall through, picture yourself having already accomplished your goals. Instead of worrying about everything that could go wrong, visualize upcoming events going right. Then "convert your dream" into reality. Here's how:

- Make a mental movie by translating a goal into a specific, well-defined image complete with color, sounds, smells, and emotions if possible.
- Put yourself into the audience and watch the movie over and over again. Visualize your goal being accomplished or an upcoming event occurring without mistakes or short-comings.
- Plant it in your subconscious. "Run" your movie right before you drop off to sleep or after you've relaxed your body and quieted your mind into a meditative state. Mentally watching your movie while engaged in a repetitive activity that doesn't require a great deal of concentration (running, riding a stationary bike, swimming laps) also works.
- As your movie "fades out," think: "I want this to happen this way, if not better!"

> "I have tremendous faith in the subconscious. I absorb all the actions I could take, submerge them in my mind, let them reform in different combinations and then recognize them as they reemerge and come into my head at three in the morning."
>
> —JEFF CUNNINGHAM
> *Associate publisher*, Forbes

Affirmations and mental movies unlock self-doubt and give you the confidence to succeed. When you visualize what you want in the above manner and are steadfast as you go after it, working hard and sticking with it, you will probably achieve it. Mike Wilfley, president of A. R. Wilfley & Sons, did. At an annual top management goal-setting meeting, Wilfley replied to the inevitable question—"How big do you want the company to be?"—by making a "mental movie" for his officers.

"Instead of giving a dollar size for the company, let me give you the feeling and a description of what is in my mind," he said. "I want a company where people feel they are industry leaders; where there are enough resources for us to stay on top of research and development; where there is enough capital for our manufacturing plant to compete with larger competitors; where we are able to maintain the wonderful, friendly, informal, family, cooperative, no back-biting atmosphere; and where each department head can be a leader who makes a difference."

As Wilfley painted that picture, everyone in the room could "see and feel" it. "It was like plugging in the Christmas lights," he later told me. "There was a glow in their eyes. They could see themselves in that role. They got involved in the group vision. There was an implicit agreement that this was damn well worth spending a career doing. They then easily ascertained the dollar amounts and timetable necessary to create the picture in their minds."

5. *Avoid being around those who are negative.* Negativity is contagious. Our negative thoughts attract negative people and experiences. "I had a bad day last Monday," a CPA once told me, "and it was so strange—everybody I met that day had a sad story to tell." Other people's negative attitudes drag us down with them as well. Negative people scare us out of doing what we want to do. They undermine our confidence by pointing out things that could go wrong. They "burst our bubbles" when we are celebrating our successes. But worst of all, they get us thinking negatively again ourselves. Spend as little time with them as possible. If you can't avoid them entirely, protect yourself with extra-positive thoughts.

6. *Expect acceptance.* A businesswoman who is four eleven and a grandmother of six is one of the handful of women in the world qualified to race funny car dragsters. She loves the reaction she gets when she pulls up to the track, jumps out of her car, and pulls off her helmet in front of a group of men.

"The guys are not pleased," she admitted. This, of course, is a colossal understatement. Usually their reaction is, "Oh, hell. It's the lady driver."

"These are huge, macho, go-crazy-on-the-track men, and I ruin their image," she said. "To get over that, I go to the track primed to expect acceptance. I get out of my car, reach out, shake their hands, and introduce myself. I'll admire the paint job on their car or their set of wheels. Then I tell them, 'Remember what your mother told you: ladies first!' 'No way! You put your helmet on. We're going to burn your butt,' is the typical response I get. That's when I know I'm in," she laughed. "I expect acceptance, and I get it."

Most of us will earn a certain amount of acceptance over time based on our performance, character, track record of achievements, and so on. But what we may not realize is that *we don't have to wait for acceptance to be granted to us*. If we want it—and all of us do—we can have it at any time, regardless of our title, age, or position. We can help ourselves to it by counting on it. All we have to do is accept ourselves and expect acceptance from others.

You can expect acceptance from anyone, anywhere, at any time, under any circumstances—*if* your attitude and self-talk convey the message that "I'm okay and you're okay too." You cannot be arrogant or demanding. You cannot have the "you owe me" attitude so often seen in bratty children or ex-spouses. Simply accept yourself. The best people to be around (and the easiest to accept) are those who are sure of their own worth. Expecting acceptance is always contingent upon first accepting yourself.

Expecting acceptance is a realistic entitlement we grant ourselves when we trust others not to hurt us and trust ourselves to handle situations in ways that earn others' respect. By calmly, quietly anticipating acceptance, we persuade others that we deserve it, and we are likely to get it. Simply put, if you expect people to accept you, they probably will. If you don't expect it, they probably won't.

7. *Finally, realize that any disposition that you do not manage ends up being managed by others—or running amok.* If you control your self-talk, you can lower your stress level, enhance your relationships, energize yourself, and influence the outcome of countless situations. So don't let emotions that arise in the heat of a moment cause you to lose the optimistic outlook you've worked so hard to find or make a decision that could adversely affect your life. Be responsible for your attitude and how you affect others. It is necessary to look optimistic even if you aren't. Either get back in control or take a breather.

TOP PEOPLE EXTEND THEIR OPTIMISTIC, ACCEPTING ATTITUDE TO OTHERS

> "I have a positive view of people. People are who they are. So, I try not to let them bother me or get under my skin, and I don't hold grudges."
>
> —JEFF SMULYAN
> *Owner, the Seattle Mariners*

Top people not only accept and have confidence in themselves, they also accept and think well of others. Unless they have evidence to the contrary, they assume that their colleagues, competitors, customers, and employees are capable, trustworthy, and just plain okay. But they are not Pollyanna-ish about it or naive or altruistic. They know that people will always try to perform at the level that is expected of them. Because chiefs expect competence, honesty, trustworthiness, and other positive qualities from others, that is what others frequently give them.

> "You're apt to find what you're looking for. You can often bring out the good qualities people ought to have by your good thoughts toward them. And if you're looking for doubt and are highly critical, you'll find

cause for that too. Harsh feelings produce harsh realities. Harsh feelings are a waste of time and a waste of energy."

—NORMAN COUSINS
Author, Anatomy of an Illness

People treat you better when you treat them well—and think well of them. Like your attitude toward yourself, your attitude toward others is evident in everything you do or don't do, say or don't say. People usually know how you feel about them—and act accordingly. If you think highly of others, you'll improve the odds that others will respond favorably to you.

When you respect others, accept them as they are, choose not to judge them, and generally view them in a favorable light, you benefit as much as they do. You appear nonjudgmental and people will feel more at ease with you. More people will do business with you because you are more likable. It removes the self-imposed stress of being on the watch to catch and correct others' faults. And you will be less defensive because you aren't thinking others are thinking poorly of you. Also, you can spend time improving yourself and advancing your career instead of wasting it mentally criticizing others.

Just as you can choose to control your thoughts about yourself, you can choose to control your thoughts about others. You are responsible for your attitude and its effects.

In time, you may forget how, when, and whom you have hurt, but your "victim" won't—not in one year, ten years, or fifty. And to quote an old adage, "what goes around, comes around." In one way or another, you pay for the harm you cause others and are rewarded for your goodwill toward them. You get back what you send out, and that principle applies to your words, your deeds—and your attitudes.

If that line of reasoning is too esoteric for you, consider the fact that in business you will not only be judged by the things you accomplish alone but also by what you motivate others to do. You will be a more effective manager (and consume a lot less time and energy) if you view people as inherently worthwhile and basically good. When you are suspicious, critical, and convinced that others will "mess up" somehow, you have to work very hard to prevent them from living down to your expectations—and it isn't really necessary to work that hard. On balance, people will accommodate your perception of them—good or bad.

How to Cultivate and Convey an Accepting Attitude Toward Others

1. *If you can't be positive, be neutral. But don't be negative.* Tolerance can tide you over until your new attitude takes hold.

There are no perfect people and there are lots of people who look at things and behave differently than you do. Every day you'll encounter individuals who disagree with, disturb, or challenge you, often making you doubt yourself in the process. As a result, you may be tempted to defend yourself by labeling such people jerks, creeps, or losers. Don't let your own insecurities prompt you to jump to those negative conclusions. And don't make snap judgments about people's motives. For one thing, until you are perfect yourself, you don't have a right to judge them. For another, what seems "wrong" to you at first glance may prove to be "right" or at least acceptable upon closer inspection.

Others have their reasons for behaving as they do. Those reasons may not be apparent immediately, but in time, you may understand others' actions and want to revise your opinion. You can—if you've remained neutral. But if you've already mentally dissected and dismissed someone, you may not get a second chance—or the opportunity to develop a relationship that could be beneficial to both of you.

2. *Consciously identify other people's positive attributes—in twenty seconds or less.* The instant your boss, spouse, neighbor, secretary, doctor, lawyer, barber, or anyone else for that matter comes into view, think of at least one good thing about that person—a talent, attractive physical feature, positive personality trait, past kindness, witty or astute comment they made . . . anything. In-depth character analysis is not required. You can practice this technique on everyone you meet, including strangers you pass on the street. It gets you into the habit of making your first thought about someone else a positive one.

3. *Don't underestimate people.* Give them 100-percent credit from the start and let them knock it down themselves if they are going to. They may not. Remember, people tend to conform to others' expectations of them. If given the opportunity, they often rise to the occasion. Even if they don't, it is easy enough for you to lower your estimation of them. Most of us have a much more difficult time changing an initially negative perception into a more positive one.

4. *Don't fool yourself into thinking that you can hide your feelings toward others. You can't.* They slip past even the friendliest façade. Your smile will seem forced. You'll speak too soon or interrupt once too often. You'll use an impatient, sarcastic, or flat, unenthusiastic tone of voice. Or a pained expression will appear on your face. In one way or another, underlying negative attitudes about people always rise to the surface and show themselves. The only way to be safe from the adverse affects of negativity toward others is to make sure you don't repeat to yourself or dwell on thoughts about anyone that you wouldn't say in exactly the same way to that person's face.

If you think I'm suggesting you force yourself to like everyone you meet, let me assure you that I am not. I do think that the number of people you choose to *dislike* should be small. However, you do not have to like someone or want that person for a friend or get a kick out of working with him to have an optimistic, accepting attitude toward him. You simply have to be positive when thinking about him.

Choose to focus on others' attributes instead of their flaws. Look for the best in them instead of the worst. Seek out similarities between yourself and the other person rather than magnifying differences. Your perception depends on your perspective.

You talk yourself into your negative opinions of people. You can talk yourself into more positive ones as well. Try assigning your mind and mentally preparing to accept others by using the following self-talk:

- "Don't speculate. Don't assume. Accept at face value. Wait and see what happens next."
- "People are generally good—even though events or conditions sometimes cause them to behave badly."
- "People's behavior rarely proves to be malicious or intentionally evil. But if it does, then I can choose not to give them another chance to hurt or disappoint me."
- "If I look for good, more often than not, I'll get it."

5. *Give compliments.* Don't just think good thoughts—say them out loud. Write notes. Send memos. Although people often sense your positive regard, they never tire of hearing you say that you think well of them. People who are told that they have your respect, trust, approval, and acceptance will work hard to keep it. Supplying that sort of positive motivation is what good management is all about. Naturally, you don't want to compliment insincerely. False flattery can backfire on you. However, if you look for things to recognize and applaud, you'll find them. Then let people know in words what you've found.

6. *Realize that positive thinking and an accepting attitude toward others does not guarantee that they will behave as we wish.* All of us have given others the benefit of the doubt only to have them turn around and take advantage of us. What's more, no matter how optimistic, effective, or skilled at relating to others we become, we will continue to be betrayed by people now and then. There will always be people in our lives who will prove that they did not merit our trust. All we can do is try not to overreact or be overly disappointed when that happens.

Bear in mind that people seldom do things because they *want to hurt you.* Much more often they are trying to *protect themselves.* Rather than attributing motives to people that they may not have ("he did that on purpose to make me look bad," or "she was getting back at me for assigning an account to someone else"), deal with the behavior. It will take some of the sting out of a painful situation.

Finally, don't let disappointments lead you to protect yourself by creating a tough outer shell of bitterness or negativity. Allowing your fear of being hurt by a few to prevent you from thinking well of others is a big mistake. It deprives you of all the wonderful opportunities and beneficial relationships that come your way when you do cultivate and convey an optimistic, accepting attitude about others.

Adopting a philosophy of optimism, increasing self-confidence, and thinking positively about yourself and others are the foundation on which business success is built. However, people who make it to the top and stay there have more than an accepting attitude going for them. The next few chapters of this book will explain that they also have the guts and smarts to translate their attitudes into effective actions.

19

"Guts"—Finding the Courage to Do What Others Don't

On the way to dinner one evening, a CEO I was interviewing (and observing in action) pulled into a boatyard in Lahaina on the Hawaiian island of Maui to inquire about renting a boat slip. It was about five-forty-five and the workday had ended, but a half dozen employees were still on the premises, standing together, drinking beer, smoking cigarettes, and talking. They were Hawaiians. We were "haoles" (a label native Hawaiians apply to nonnatives, especially the white American mainland variety). They saw us drive in but ignored us.

While I waited in the car (where I could watch the following scene unfold), the CEO walked up to the workers, smiled, and asked, "Does anyone know who I can talk to about renting a boat slip?" He received no answer and, in fact, no response at all. The men completely ignored him.

He repeated his question. This time, one of the men grunted, "None available."

The CEO persisted. "When there *are* slips available, how much do they go for?" he inquired.

By this time all six men were glaring at the CEO in a decidedly unfriendly manner, but one of them grudgingly replied, "Three hundred fifty dollars a month."

"Hell, I don't want to rent a condo, I want to rent a boat slip," said the CEO, attempting to use a bit of humor. Although not rip-roaringly funny, his remark briefly brought smiles to several men's faces. But almost immediately the workers turned away again, resuming their private conversations, as if the CEO were not there.

But he did not go away. Instead he asked to bum a cigarette. "Smoking etiquette" compelled one of the smokers to give the CEO a cigarette. As he took it and said "thanks" he briefly grasped the shoulder of the man who had done him a favor by supplying the cigarette. Then he asked a different worker for a light and steadied the man's hand with his own while accepting the light. (He had now physically insinuated himself into their group by making physical contact with two of its members.)

After the cigarette was lit, the CEO took a big drag and coughed. He mentioned that the cigarette was stronger than the brand he smoked. "Mine only have half the stuff that kills you," he joked. He revealed that his kids were constantly harping on him to quit. "They're afraid I'm going to die of cancer," he said. Two of the men nodded in understanding. They had relatives who worried about their health too.

Soon after that personal connection had been made, one of the workers offered the CEO some information: "The only way to get a boat slip around here is to get a boat from this yard and make sure you get the slip as part of the deal."

The CEO asked if any boats were for sale. They pointed one out to him, and he asked, "How much?" As prices were being discussed, one man offered the CEO a beer. He accepted it and knew the ice was broken. He had won them over. The next day we went back for a test ride in the boat, and he was greeted by the workers as if he were an old buddy.

Under the same circumstances, could *you* have done what that CEO did? Even if you were well versed in and comfortable with asking favors, getting personal, and the other techniques you've read about and the CEO used, could you have continued to use them after you'd failed to elicit a favorable response not once but several times? Or would you have given up early on, perhaps as soon as you realized that the boatyard was closed for business or saw that the workers were anything but interested in conversing with you?

Most people would have walked away after hearing that no boat slips were available or packed it in when their first stab at humor didn't noticeably reduce the tension. As a result, they would not have obtained the information they had come to get.

That CEO was not like most people. He *was* like other top people, however. He achieved his objective because, even in an unfriendly, at times hostile, situation he had the *guts* to:

- initiate;
- act;
- persevere;
- endure;
- take chances;
- risk failure;
- try again or try something else when what he did proved unsuccessful.

WHAT ARE GUTS?

Guts are a combination of confidence, courage, conviction, strength of character, stick-to-it-iveness, pugnaciousness, backbone, and intestinal fortitude. They are mandatory for anyone who wants to get to and stay at the top.

People who don't have them are relegated to the role of "yes men." They play it safe, limit their potential, and must settle for the position of "follower" for the duration of their careers. As they say: no guts, no glory.

In business, courage is called for dozens of times every day. You need guts to:

- tell someone his business is in trouble;
- disagree with your boss, peers, or customers;
- speak up when you see that something isn't being done correctly;
- question or challenge policies or practices you believe are unfair or unsafe;
- admit you don't have all the answers and ask for advice;
- reprimand or terminate employees;
- make potentially unpopular decisions;
- walk into any meeting, sales situation, or lecture hall where even a remote possibility of "falling flat on your face" exists.

Top people have the courage to do those things and then some. "I break rules that don't make sense. Fire me or get out of the way." Like the CEO who made this declaration, some chiefs are unmistakably gutsy. Their self-confident "ready-to-rise-to-any-challenge" presence practically precedes them into a room. Yet they are rarely if ever arrogant, brash, overly aggressive, obnoxious, or "devil-may-care" in attitude or action. Indeed, some are exactly the opposite. They convey their inner strength and gutsiness in a calm, reassuring, almost soothing manner.

> "One can be courageous in a quiet, gentlemanly way. Sometimes a modest posture gets the best results."
> —**HOWARD SOLOMON**
> *President, Forest Laboratories*

People who have guts *are not merely thrill seekers*. Although they will risk failure for a chance at success, they do not take risks just for a rush of excitement. *Neither are they belligerent or hostile*. They have the courage to say what's on their minds and handle confrontations. But, they do not go looking for fights, back people into corners and attack them for sport, "blast" people for making mistakes, or even take advantage of every opportunity to confront others.

They are not impulsive or hot-headed. They think on their feet, rather than reacting without thinking. They have the courage to be spontaneous when spontaneity is called for, but you'll never catch them diving into a pool without first checking the depth (and maybe even the temperature) of the water.

Finally, people who have guts *are not free of fears.* What separates people with guts from those without them is not fearlessness but the willingness to deal with their fears and do what needs to be done nonetheless.

SITUATIONAL COURAGE

Situational courage comes from confidence in yourself and your ideas. "Self-assurance based on a foundation of knowledge and experience, the initiative to take calculated risks," is the way one CEO describes it. It requires different kinds of "intestinal fortitude" to take:

- *physical risks* (sky diving, rock climbing, running a marathon);
- *social risks* (go on a blind date, initiate conversations at a cocktail party);
- *accuracy risks* (go against the norm, challenge a long-standing assumption);
- or *popularity risks* (discipline or terminate an employee, support a controversial cause, institute budget cuts).

And all of us—chiefs included—have more guts in some of those situations than in others. In the areas we have successfully met challenges, already conquered our fears, or naturally feel at ease, we have *situational courage.* However, the challenges posed by the business world are a combination of physical, social, accuracy, and popularity risks, and those of us who are serious about moving up in an organization have to accept whatever challenges come our way—not just the ones we feel comfortable facing. We have to take the necessary risks—not just the easy ones.

In addition to the situational courage we already have, we need to find the courage to initiate, the courage of our convictions, the courage to make decisions, and the courage to make mistakes. As Steve Murrin, partner in Billy Bob's Texas, puts it, "You can stay a big fish in a small pond or jump in a bigger pond and get to be a bigger fish (at the risk of getting eaten)."

THE COURAGE TO INITIATE

"Take action. You never know what part in your life the phone call you return will play—even when you don't even know the person you're calling. You never know who will sit next to you on the airplane and where your conversation may lead. You never know who's going to see your name mentioned in the local paper. Make sure you don't make an ass out of yourself because you never know with whom you're dealing. But *don't wait* . . . because you never know."

—**BILL DANIELS**
Chairman, Daniels Communications

If you want to get to the top, you cannot wait for others to show you the way or make you feel comfortable. You have to initiate. Speak up. Take action. Make the first move. Nothing much happens unless we initiate. A great deal happens when we do.

• I had long admired and enjoyed the work of a nationally syndicated columnist and one day got up the nerve to initiate a telephone call to introduce myself to him. "I like your style," I began and then said, "I'm sure you're approached with ideas all the time, but I think I have developed a unique niche for myself. Would you be interested in talking to me about it some time?" He said he would call me back and was true to his word. The next day he returned my call. We talked for an hour, and the following week, there was a full column about me in the *Chicago Tribune* (which was then syndicated to sixty-odd papers around the country). The very same day that article appeared, *Newsweek* and *Time* magazine both telephoned me to do a story.

• I was in Hong Kong, heading to Bangkok, Thailand, when I initiated a conversation with a man waiting for the same plane. As it turned out, that man controlled 70 percent of the world's rice, owned forty companies, and was headed to Bangkok to buy Thailand's rice. He agreed to be interviewed for this book, and we talked all the way to Bangkok. The next day he telephoned to invite me to sit in on a normally closed-door meeting with four of his company presidents from India, Hong Kong, Australia, and England so that I could observe their negotiations with Thailand's minister of agriculture and other government officials.

• Thirteen years ago, one of my two best friends moved to India. Ever since, I've wondered whether she was still alive, how she was doing, and what she was doing, but I never heard a word from her. Then while living in New York doing research for this book, I initiated a conversation in an elevator (which, as you may know, is something most people in New York don't do). I turned to a very attractive, familiar-looking woman who was in the elevator with a man and myself and said, "You are very pretty. And it's amazing how much you look like an old friend of mine." She smiled politely. I continued, "My friend was from Haiti." She commented, "Well, I'm from Haiti." I told her, "My friend's name is Raphie Venturi." She looked at me and said, "She's my sister." What an opportunity I would have lost to meet this person (and find out about my friend Raphie) had I not initiated that conversation!

Top people initiate. Their own success *and* the success of their companies depend on it. CEOs, COOs, chairmen of the board, and company presidents don't have the luxury of sitting back and waiting for others to act so they can respond. If they did that, businesses would have no leaders, only caretakers. There would never be any change or improvement or innovation. Everything that happens in the business world (and elsewhere) happens because someone initiates it.

What Happens When You Initiate?

1. *You have a better chance of staying on top of any situation.* Although you may not actually control interactions, you at least start them moving in the direction of your choice and usually improve the odds that their outcomes will be beneficial to you.

2. *You'll likely receive support.* More often than not, people will respond favorably when you break the ice or take the lead. They may even have wanted to start the conversation or bring up the point you did, but were afraid to do it.

3. *You avoid falling victim to a "herd" instinct.* The "I-have-to-do-it-this-way-because-everyone-else-does" mentality maintains the status quo even when the status quo is mediocrity. Like a lemming, you can blindly follow all the other lemmings right over the edge of the cliff. Or you can initiate, present your ideas at the outset and have others follow *your* lead.

4. *You also make your own luck.* Good fortune is not just "strokes of luck" serendipitously bestowed upon you because "somebody up there" likes you. Good luck is more often the result of recognizing an opportunity and taking advantage of it—by initiating.

Several years ago, I stopped at a restaurant on my way to the airport, hoping to get a bite to eat in the little time I had before catching my plane. Unfortunately, the hostess said there would be a twenty-minute wait for a table. Since I couldn't afford to wait, I smiled pleasantly and walked past her into the restaurant to look for a recently seated party who had a spare seat at their table and might not mind if I sat with them. I soon spotted three men seated at a table for four, walked over to them and said, "I know this sounds strange but I have to catch a plane and I can't wait for a table of my own. Would you mind if I took this seat?" Although they were visibly surprised by my unusual request, they agreed. We introduced ourselves, and I learned that they were with a company whose president I had met the year before in Antigua. At the end of the meal, we exchanged business cards and they said they would mention to the president that they had met me. They did, and I subsequently received two speaking assignments from their company.

Yes, it was a "lucky coincidence" that those men worked for someone I knew. But I was "lucky" to meet them because I had the guts to initiate.

It's amazing how many opportunities we miss simply because we are afraid to make the first move. We are afraid that others will ignore or reject or laugh at us. We worry about being wrong or misunderstood or perceived as pushy and intrusive. Yet taking the initiative almost always brings positive results. Others not only accept and respond to you favorably but also often appreciate and even admire your courage. In fact, they were probably thinking, "Gee, it would be nice if someone broke the ice," or "I wish someone would make a joke. You could cut the tension in here with a knife," or "I don't understand a word that man is saying. It sure would help if someone asked him for some specific examples." Well, *you* can be the one to do it.

The ball is in your court. Don't give it away. Tell yourself, "I have the ball. I own it and I'm going to score as many points as I possibly can with it!" Then initiate, initiate, initiate. The courage to initiate is one of the major differences between those who make it and those who don't.

When Should You Initiate?

Always, but especially when most people wouldn't. For example:

• Most candidates go into *job interviews*, shake hands, perhaps make small talk (or more likely respond to the interviewer's small talk), and then wait for the first question. Instead, take the initiative. Say something like, "There's a lot we can talk about today. Would you like to start?" The interviewer was going to start anyway, but with that simple, low-key statement, you've already set yourself apart from the rest of the candidates he or she will interview.

• At some point in any job interview, it's inevitable that you will be asked how much you want to be paid. When it comes to *salary negotiations*, if you wait to be asked, no matter how you respond, you risk being too high or too low and hurting your chances of going further. Instead of waiting for that uncomfortable question and then fumbling around for the best answer you can come up with, bring up the subject first. One way to do that might be to say, "Money is not my main consideration, but I'm curious—what is the salary range you've budgeted for this position?" By initiating this or any other part of your conversation, you'll have more (although not total) control over the outcome.

• As you advance in your field, you're likely to be interviewed on television or by newspaper and magazine writers. Because *media interviews* tend to be particularly stressful conversations, most of us have a tendency to let the interviewer take the lead and keep it throughout. That's a major mistake. Your only hope of influencing the direction of a television interview or what gets printed about you in an article is by taking the initiative. At the first available opportunity, grab the reins and say, "What your audience might be interested in" or "One point I'd like to bring up" and pursue the topics *you* want covered. If that sounds too cheeky, it may help to know that Johnny Carson says the best guests on his show are the ones who take the initiative.

• Like many people, you may not like *business socializing*, but the fact is you have to do it. By initiating, you can make yourself feel comfortable, and, just as important, make others feel comfortable. If you're the one launching the exchange, they can relax, and as they do, they become more receptive to you. So, initiate conversation. Volunteer information about yourself. Ask questions. Maintain a friendly facial expression. Volunteer your full name before the other person does—even if you are well known. If you've forgotten the other person's name, by saying yours first, you'll get theirs in response.

• *When meeting new people*, initiate handshakes and conversations. Don't wait until someone extends his or her hand to you. Regardless of your sex or theirs, your position or theirs, or how long you've known them, be first to offer your hand. Start conversations with people at the bar or at the buffet table, people in a group, or people standing alone. Bob Hunter, president of Pepsi-Co Food Systems, says a major consideration in deciding whom he'll promote "is the person's interpersonal skills: the willingness to go up and meet new people and introduce himself rather than just staying with cronies."

• And, of course, taking the initiative is essential for *selling* anything. The problem is that most salespeople initiate the wrong things. They come in full of energy and proceed to *tell* potential customers why they should buy their product or service. As explained in chapter 17, asking questions is the more effective way to initiate a sales call.

Nothing happens unless someone initiates. Although there's no guarantee you'll get everything you want by initiating, I *can* guarantee that you'll get less (or nothing at all) if you don't. So, get out there and get friendly quickly. You may not get another chance. Speak up, ask a question, offer a suggestion—when the opportunity arises. Take the risk now because later may be *too* late.

While working in Greece, I observed a man approaching apparent strangers and striking up conversations with them. When one group of "new friends" moved on, he'd find another. Finally, I approached him and asked why he was so freely initiating conversations with strangers. "Because I know the opportunity may never come again," he replied.

THE COURAGE OF YOUR CONVICTIONS

"Courage to follow through on your own convictions is critical. You can test out your opinions on others, but once you have, you are the one who must decide what to do and whether or not to do it—and that takes courage. Our society is full of Monday morning quarterbacks—people who have all the answers after the fact. You need real courage at those times when you're sitting alone, thinking things through (and deciding what you are going to do next)."

—**EINAR KLOSTER**
President and CEO, Philips Lighting Hold B.V.

When you have "the courage of your convictions," you do what *you* know is right. Although most of the top people I interviewed would not necessarily come right out and call themselves courageous, the word describes every one of them. They have the guts to stand firm and conduct themselves and their business dealings in what they believe to be the right, proper, correct, or best possible way. They communicate their convictions and act upon them—even when others might not agree with their position and even when they realize there's a chance that they could end up being wrong.

"Of course, they do," you may be thinking. "When you're the boss, you can do things any way you want. You don't have a supervisor breathing down your neck or one who will fire you in a flash or keep you on but make your office hours a living hell. Even if people disagree with Mr. Big, they're not going to shout him down in a meeting or make him a laughingstock or give him the silent treatment for weeks or months on end."

While all of that may be true, you will still be better off in the long run if you *don't* do what most people do—blindly follow all instructions (including those that you know will lead to calamity or that you are morally opposed to) and never propose alternatives that could improve upon the way things have always been done.

What you think is best based on your experience, training, education, values, and instincts may in fact be the best way to go. It may save time or money. It may prevent accidents or remedy morale problems or generate favorable publicity. And it could draw positive attention to you—along with promotions and bonuses. But you'll never know (and neither will anyone else) unless you find the courage to speak up, speak out, and take a stand. Referring to cable limited partnerships and to Mind Extension University (ME/U), a cable television "University" he founded, Glenn R. Jones, CEO of Jones Intercable, Inc., recalls, "No one thought they were good ideas—not the bankers or the businesspeople. But I did—and they were."

Having the courage of your convictions is NOT rebelling against authority. Although the words "you can't" have motivated many of us to achieve goals others said were impossible, kicking up a fuss every time your superiors veto your plans or insist that you do things their way is a sign of immaturity, not guts.

Nor do you want to be a rabble-rouser. People with the courage of their convictions don't hold gripe sessions around the water cooler or start a protest movement whenever they think they have been treated unfairly or hope their superiors will have a change of heart. Make sure you are taking a stand and not just overreacting to a disappointment.

To speak up, speak out, and take a stand effectively:

- Be willing, able, and prepared to explain and defend your position.
- Consider the consequences (without letting fear or the need to show you're not afraid cloud your thinking). Most business-related convictions are not a matter of life or death. There will be times when it is best not to make an issue of being right. Realistically look at what you stand to gain or lose by taking a stand—and act accordingly.
- Keep an open mind. As the following anecdote illustrates, *your* right way is not necessarily the only right way to do something.

I had been working on a project with one of the people I interviewed for this book and continued on without him when he left the room to take a telephone call. Upon his return, he took a look at what I had done and asked me to organize it differently. "Sorry," I said, "I didn't realize I was doing it incorrectly."

"You weren't," he said. "You just did it differently than I would have done it. *It's not my way right.*"

I asked him to elaborate, and he explained that he tells his employees there are four ways to do anything:

1. my way right;
2. your way right;
3. my way wrong; and
4. your way wrong.

He defined "my way right" as solving problems in the manner *his* experience, education, values, and instincts have taught him. From his perspective, it's the right way.

"Your way right," he said, "is when you solve problems or make decisions based on what your experience, education, values, and instincts have taught you. From where *you* stand, it's the right way. Since no two people have had exactly the same experiences, 'my way right' and 'your way right' will usually differ."

He went on to explain that "doing something 'my way wrong' " is choosing a solution even though it seems incorrect to others. He might even realize it's not the right direction himself, he told me, but he goes with it anyway because it's what he wants or, in his opinion, it's still the best option available.

Finally, "your way wrong" is planning to solve a problem in a certain way even though you know it's not right and the boss knows it's not right. Why would anyone ever choose that option? Out of ignorance or spite.

"In a company, any problem can be handled with the first, second, or third approach," he concluded. "The fourth should not be tolerated."

If you are the boss and you delegate a project, you can expect it to be done "their way right" (the second option)—unless you explain that you want it done your way right (the first option)—and are clear about what that entails. Understanding this helps you tell the difference between a mistake and a difference of opinion so you can deal with either one appropriately.

As a subordinate being delegated a specific responsibility, it is best not to proceed directly to your right way. But you do not have to second-guess or try to please your boss by doing only what you think he wants either. You may guess wrong or come off as an ingratiating apple polisher. Instead come back with a Plan A and a Plan B based on your experience, training, values, and instincts and be able to explain and defend both. Although you risk being wrong, chances are that your boss—after making a few suggestions or revisions—will accept one of your plans. Even if he doesn't, you'll learn something about the way he likes things done that you can use to your advantage in the future and have developed more courage. The next time you want or need to present your ideas to others or stand up for something you believe in, it won't be as scary as it once was.

THE COURAGE TO MAKE DECISIONS

"There is a huge difference between being number one and being number two. Number one is a decision maker."

—MARSHALL LOEB
Managing editor, Fortune

You get to be number one by having the courage to:

- *probe* for all the facts you need to make a well-informed decision;
- *listen* to other people's opinions—even the ones that make it more difficult to make a decision;
- *examine* all of the alternatives and consider the unconventional and unpopular ones as well as the one that seemed best to you right off the bat;
- *file* away the information you've gathered just in case Plan A fails and you have to switch to Plan B;
- *act*—make the decision and deal with its aftermath.

It takes courage to make decisions because there's always a fifty-fifty chance that any decision will be the wrong decision. Most people are afraid of being wrong. They conjure up old images of big red X's beside the incorrect answers on test papers (and big red F's at the top of the page), of parents angrily shouting over "spilled milk" or looking horribly disappointed about some other wrongdoing, of peers laughing when the wrong thing had been said or teammates blaming them for a game lost because of the fly ball they misjudged and failed to catch. They think they can reduce the odds of being wrong (and avoid feelings of failure, embarrassment, or humiliation) by reducing the number of decisions they make.

Successful people know that there is also a fifty-fifty chance that any decision will be the right decision. They boost their confidence by reminding themselves that they are probably going to be right at least half of the time. And they recognize that the cost of making the wrong decision will never be as high as the cost of *indecision*.

When you don't make decisions:

- other people will, and their choices may not work out as favorably for you as your own;
- unsolved problems get worse;
- unresolved conflicts reoccur;
- you look wishy-washy, insecure, and as if you are not willing to get pinned down or "take the ball and run with it"—none of which does anything to show the powers that be that you have executive presence or could handle executive responsibility.

To help you avoid those consequences (and drum up some courage), here's a short course in decision making.

1. *Be willing to make the necessary decisions.* During any business day, you are likely to find yourself in countless situations that require you to make decisions. It doesn't take a great deal of courage to make the decisions you want to make (to break for lunch, read a business journal, stop by a colleague's office for a friendly chat). You won't have trouble making "easy" decisions either. It is the necessary decisions—the ones with the most riding on them, the ones that have to be made by a certain time or date, and the ones that others are watching you make (to see how you do it or figure out whether or not to support you) that are the most difficult (and the most important) to make. Recognize which decisions are important and devote the lion's share of your time and energy to making them. It may be human nature to put off the big decisions for as long as you can and blame your indecisiveness on all the other matters you had to attend to first. But *you* don't have to be superhuman to overcome that tendency.

2. *Strive for a calm attitude,* not a macho or desperate "surrounded by the enemy" stance. Sometimes a crisis will be the factor that motivates you to make a decision, but even under those circumstances, a calm, in-control presence is essential.

3. *Gather facts and opinions from as many sources as possible to get as many varying points of view as possible.* Read, consult experts, and try to look at the situation from the perspectives of everyone actually involved in it. Don't just guess. Go to the source and ask for input. Open-mindedly listen to those who disagree with you as well as those who support you. Probe, probe, probe.

4. *Distill the information you've gathered.* Consider as many alternatives as possible. Have Plan A, Plan B, Plan C, and so on. Know the potential costs and benefits of each.

5. *Listen to your intuition.* Not all decisions are made solely on the basis of fact. Sometimes a gut feeling or a hunch makes one option more appealing than another.

If the facts, your intuition, or a combination of the two still do not point to a clear-cut way to go, you're simply going to have to take a chance. More than one major business decision has come down to the flip of the coin. However, the chance you take simply may be to go with the lesser of two evils or make a decision you suspect is the wrong one and repair the damage at a later date.

"Don't overwork the decision-making process," Neil Georgi, president of Georgi & Associates, advises. "Have a *reasonable* amount of fact, and then act."

6. *When you can, reduce the pressure caused by deadlines or the need to make on-the-spot decisions.* Normally time causes the most pressure. Worrying about missing a deadline can often push you into making premature decisions or faulty ones. If time constraints are so severe that you have to decide before you feel confident about your decision, the best decision is apt to be a "no." Generally you can change your mind later.

7. *If time permits and it is appropriate, set the decision aside for later consideration.* Sometimes time or changing circumstances alleviates the need for a decision (a "problem" employee you thought you'd have to fire may quit). Sometimes no decision is a decision (by refusing to side with either feuding party in your department you are deciding to let them work out their differences on their own).

Or turn it over to your subconscious. Think about the problem before falling to sleep or engaging in an unrelated activity. Even though your conscious mind is not focused on it, your subconscious is still working on the problem, mulling it over, and factoring in data you had buried or forgotten. When you consciously come back to the subject, you will have a fresh perspective on it and, in some instances, instinctively know which decision to make.

> "If I'm faced with a difficult situation, I might go and do some form of aerobic exercise. I don't actually think about the letter, interview, speech, or whatever was on my mind previously. Yet, when I finish exercising, I'll know what I need to do or what I'm going to say."
>
> —BILL COORS
> *Chairman, Adolph Coors Company*

8. *Make the decision.* If you encounter a stumbling block, talk with the necessary people, but don't talk to them as if you are asking for their permission or approval.

Keep in mind that no matter what the decision some won't like the outcome. (Firing John Smith may be a good decision for the company. His replacement will be happy about it and his former subordinates may be too. But rarely will Mr. and Mrs. Smith think it's a good decision.)

> "I had to fire a department manager. After I did it, I called my boss and told him what I had done. When

he said I couldn't do that, I said, 'I knew you'd say that. That's why I told you after I did it.' "

—**ERNIE HOWELL**
Retired president, St. Regis/WPM

A CEO told me: "People can't feel you're equivocating. I make decisions fast and I communicate those decisions." *The higher up the corporate ladder you go, the more "big" decisions you'll have to make.* More people will be affected by your decisions. More people will be watching you make them. In addition, the information you need to make the decision gets filtered through more people before it gets to you. All of this makes decision making more difficult—even if you do have the advantage of seeing the total picture, delegating the responsibility for executing the decision to someone else, or deciding to pass the decision making back downward.

9. *If the decision is wrong, say "oops" and take corrective action.* Authority and responsibility must wear the same pair of shoes. If the decision doesn't work, a good boss takes the responsibility. If it does work a good boss passes credit around.

THE COURAGE TO MAKE MISTAKES

An amusing anecdote I've heard more than once has a junior executive conversing with a senior executive:
"How did you get to be so successful?" the junior executive asks.
"By making good decisions," the senior executive replies.
"But, how did you learn to make good decisions?"
"From experience."
"And how did you get experience?"
"By making bad decisions."
Fact: If you make decisions, you're going to make mistakes.
Falsehood: Making a mistake will spell the end of your career.

The truth is that making mistakes is not the tragedy many of us think it is. Truly successful people can point out plenty of mistakes they made along the way, and many of them take pride in the accomplishments that came as a direct or indirect result of their mistakes. Top people do not stop trying after they make mistakes. They do not stop taking risks so they can avoid making mistakes. They just try not to make the *same* mistakes over and over again.

> "Every succeeding mistake must be a mistake of a different kind. You shouldn't make the same mistake twice. And you don't when you admit them to yourself and face up to yourself."
>
> —GORDON PARKER
> *Chairman, president, and CEO,*
> *Newmont Mining Corporation*

Although you don't want to and certainly shouldn't try to, you can expect to make mistakes. Everybody does.

> "I can look back at some real foul-ups. I was in professional trouble more than once in my life."
>
> —STEWART BLAIR
> *CEO, United Artists Entertainment Company*

The trick is not to allow your mistakes to defeat you.

> "Successful people are not 'risk aversive' . . . there is a correlation between high achievement and the willingness to take risks. We are all going to have setbacks, but we can't let the prospect of failure deter us."
>
> —TOM JORDAN
> *Owner, Jordan Vineyards*

Successful people don't abandon their ambitions or lose their enthusiasm because of some odd boner. Even when others seem to be reveling over their mistakes—as competitors, underlings, and superiors who feel threatened by up-and-coming "hotshots" often do—they are not discouraged from continuing toward their goals. They still risk being wrong and, as a result, learn that not only can they recover from their mistakes but they also can go on to higher levels of achievement.

> "I'm truly a survivor. The setbacks in business were turning points."
>
> —CAROLYNE ROEHM
> *President, Carolyne Roehm, Inc.*

It's actually a mistake not to make mistakes. No one is perfect—and most of us don't trust or feel comfortable with anyone who appears to be without flaws.

> "When I'm evaluating a job candidate, I get suspicious if he looks *too* good. If I see no failures, I assume he's had it too easy."
>
> —W. RICHARD KERN
> *Managing partner, Heidrick and Struggles, Inc.*

Chiefs get to make their own mistakes—and take full responsibility for them. At lower levels of the corporation, you may be in a position to make other people's mistakes as well as your own. Your boss's poor judgment or your peers' failure to follow through on their share of the project can make you look bad. You can still learn from the mistake, but you won't if you waste your time and energy on pointing the finger and blaming others for the mess all of you are in. No matter who's at fault, you are responsible for what you do about mistakes after they are made—gripe about them or learn from them and move on.

> "If you make a mistake, a real faux pas, you should: Admit it. Apologize if you've offended. Take responsibility for it. Don't try to hide it. Don't try to make excuses. Don't do it again."
>
> —LODWRICK COOK
> *Chairman and CEO, ARCO*

And when dealing with an employee who has made a mistake—

> "If you berate him in front of people, you'll lose every-
> thing. Take him into your office. Explain the error that
> has been made and how it occurred. Then encourage
> him to go on. That way, you create loyalty (instead of
> resentment)."
>
> —JOSEPH V. VITTORIA
> *Chairman and CEO, Avis, Inc.*

One of life's ironies is that young people are afraid to make
mistakes and older people wish they had made more of them.
They look back on their lives and realize that the biggest mistake
they made was the mistake of being too careful. In retrospect
they see that they and others would have benefitted if they had
spent less time avoiding situations that might lead to mistakes
and more time taking chances, making mistakes, and learning
from them.

Our slipups are almost never career ending or life threatening.
What's more, one of the strange but true facts of life is that no
matter how horrifying or humiliating a mistake seems when we
make it, one day we'll look back and laugh at it. That day may
be a long time coming, but it will arrive.

It has taken years, but I can now laugh at the horrendously
poor judgment I used in an attempt to make a point with one
company president. I sent him two hundred withered flowers,
one for each person he had to terminate. I attached a note that
read, "Just as these flowers could be revived, your employees
could be revived with my career consulting advice." Needless
to say, my ploy backfired. It bombed completely. I was black-
balled from his company. But the world did not end. Four years
later (and after his retirement) I had the opportunity to meet
with that company president over lunch, and apologies were
made and accepted.

I would not use the foregoing approach again. I learned not
to make *that* mistake. But I did not allow it to stop me from
initiating, taking a stand, making decisions, or taking different

risks in other situations. You simply cannot get to the top or stay there if you allow the discomfort a potential blunder might cause you to keep you from doing what needs to be done.

Like my error, yours may reflect poor judgment, but it also reflects your willingness to take risks—and leaders take risks.

HOW TO BECOME MORE COURAGEOUS

1. *Initiate. Initiate. Initiate.* Get into the habit, and you'll get good at it. Practice making the first move by:

* collecting a late payment in person;
* sending a brief letter to a business leader you'd like to meet and following it up with a telephone call;
* volunteering to give a speech;
* thanking someone in writing for a job well done;
* sending a congratulatory note to someone you read about in the newspaper;
* contacting someone who's angry with you and trying to resolve the disagreement;
* telephoning someone you've fired to see how he's doing.

2. *Work on a particular area in which you are weak or feel uncomfortable* (making "cold" telephone contacts, initiating conversations at cocktail parties, asking questions when you're in a group and might look "dumb," etc). At the next available opportunity to do something in that area, make at least three attempts to do it before you give up on trying. You make progress in direct proportion to your willingness to confront the problem.

3. *Make a list of things that are difficult or anxiety provoking for you and, on a daily basis, attempt to conquer one of the items on that personal "scary-things-to-do list."* Again, don't give up until you've tried at least three times.

4. *Just forge ahead and take the appropriate risks.* No matter how nervous you feel, do what needs to be done anyway. As one man I know likes to say, "If you're at the washing machine, put in the dirty laundry."

5. *Have faith.* The execution may be awkward, but usually the outcome will still be good. Simply trust that axiom to prove true and jump in. At times, faith and an "ignorance-is-bliss" courage enables you to accomplish successfully things that you never would have attempted if you sat down beforehand and thought about how difficult they could be.

6. *Don't panic.* Most of us sound the alarm and push the panic button before we've figured out if there really is cause for alarm. Don't conclude that the world as you know it is about to end until you've thought things through. Most situations are not as bad as they look at first glance.

20

"Smarts"—Developing and Communicating Competence

Competence may not be all you need for business success, but you do need it—along with the *smarts* to continue to increase and communicate it.

Having smarts is not the same as being smart. A high grade-point average does not necessarily translate into a CEO position.

> "Brightness never took anybody to the top. Today's business leaders didn't have perfect SAT scores."
> —**J. RICHARD MUNRO**
> *Cochairman and co-CEO, Time Warner, Inc.*

By their own admission, chiefs are not always the smartest people in their organizations. And many truly brilliant individuals aren't successful at all. Their intelligence may hold them back when they rely on it exclusively and don't develop the managerial and people skills to go with their sharp minds. "Super intelligence" without a basic understanding of human nature and the ability to look at situations emotionally as well as analytically often grinds proceedings to a halt instead of making things happen. Or as one boss said about a financial "whiz kid" he supervised, "He's so brilliant, he won't amount to anything more."

Top people often *hire* brilliance. They surround themselves with people whose intellectual capacities exceed their own so that they have more than their own brain power to draw on when tackling complex problems. Now, *that's* having smarts.

Smarts are a combination of basic intelligence, know-how, shrewdness, people skills, and business acumen. They are a core competence that results from mixing technical expertise with personal effectiveness. When you have smarts your mind can soar, but your head is rarely in the clouds. Your creativity is tempered by common sense. Your interest in exploring new possibilities is balanced by practicality and the realities of any situation in which you find yourself.

PEOPLE WITH SMARTS

1. *They are open-minded and flexible about their objectives and how to accomplish them.* They look for new insights and other people's input about existing problems or upcoming projects. Although they are not wishy-washy or indecisive, they *are* willing to change their minds if someone shows them a better way to build a mousetrap.

2. *Smarts people are people-wise.* They understand human nature and have the know-how to motivate others to excel. As a result, their strategies are effectively and enthusiastically executed by the people they manage.

3. *They know their field and the people in it.* They are familiar with every aspect of their organization and are deeply involved in it. Although they have access to technical and managerial advisers and draw upon their expertise as needed, they do not rely on such advice alone.

4. *Part of having smarts is also having an insatiable thirst for knowledge.* As far as they're concerned, what they already know is never enough. They keep searching for new information, new ideas, and other ways to be more competent and communicate their competence to others.

> "I have a real curiosity about things and passionately pursue detailed know-how. . . . I can't conceive of not knowing . . . my search for knowledge is unrelenting . . . knowledge gives you freedom. . . . I don't understand people who don't want to know. . . . I want to be someone others would go over a mountain pass with in a snowstorm."
>
> —CAROLYNE ROEHM
> *President, Carolyne Roehm, Inc.*

Naturally, it's impossible to know everything about everything or even everything about any particular subject. However, people with smarts are willing to learn as much as possible. What's more, they have the ability to figure out what they need to know in a given situation and where to look for that information.

> "I buy up to six hundred dollars' worth of books at a time from places like the World Future Society. I keep three backpacks of books nearby at all times—one at the office, one at home, and one in the airplane. Reading is raking in ideas. It may not always generate new ideas, but it allows me to take in and orchestrate ideas that are already floating around."
>
> —GLENN R. JONES
> *CEO, Jones Intercable, Inc.*

People with smarts take time to think. They think to solve problems, make plans, and get results. They also think for sport, for diversion, and for the sheer joy of pondering life's endless possibilities and considering life's abundant absurdities.

On one of my business trips, I had the opportunity to meet

and talk with the president of an international company that remanufactures used parts for vehicles in Third World countries. He circumnavigates the globe once a month. "With such a limited amount of personal time, what do you do for fun?" I asked.

Without a second's hesitation, he replied, "I think."

When it comes to business, top people do not just aimlessly ponder and postulate. As the late Norman Cousins, author of *Anatomy of an Illness*, put it, they "think and ink." Successful people think and then organize their thoughts into plans of action. They assimilate the information they gather and use it to accomplish their objectives. If they did not think effectively, they wouldn't be able to do their jobs. Likewise, if they didn't put their thoughts into action, their smarts would be wasted. Top people *think to do*, do, and then think about what they've done.

Most of us prefer to work for bosses whom we consider to be intelligent. But we don't make that determination based solely on the diplomas we see hanging on their walls. Although formal education *is* important and most chiefs would encourage others to get as much of it as they can, what they look for in the people they hire and promote as well as what we look for in the people we want as leaders is *effective* intelligence. Effective intelligence is a combination of:

- book smarts;
- street smarts;
- a willingness to keep acquiring more information;
- the ability to use the information you have constructively and communicate your ideas to others clearly.

Getting ahead in business (and in life) is not a matter of how many cylinders we have. It's the result of how many we use and how we use them. Putting the basic intelligence we have to good use (thinking, organizing information into fully formed ideas, conveying those ideas to others, following through, and so on) is preferable to having more intellectual ability but not knowing how to use it effectively. You don't have to be a genius in order to make a lot of money or make it to the top in your chosen field. You do have to get as much mileage as possible from what you know (or can find out) about your field and the people in it.

THINK MORE AND THINK CREATIVELY

Most of what we do, we do without thinking. In fact, my research has shown that most people spend less than 20 percent of their time thinking versus 80 percent of their time doing.

Why? Because in our busy world, there are so many distractions, so many people to talk to, so many things to do, that we are left with very little time to think—and we don't make time for thinking. In addition, much of what we do is so patterned and well learned that little conscious thought is necessary—and we don't make the extra effort to think about what we are doing. We act out of habit, repeating the same old behaviors even though new ones might be more effective. We act without awareness and, as a result, have less control over our behavior, its effects, and our careers.

It takes effort to think anything through, and it requires even more time and energy to think the way top people do. However, the alternative is to get stuck in old, ineffective thought patterns, or worse yet, to stop thinking for ourselves altogether and let others do our thinking for us, dictating and policing our beliefs and behavior. To avoid those consequences and to get smarts, try the following fresh, new approaches to thinking.

1. *Practice simple, straightforward, sequential thinking.* Pick an issue—wanting a pay raise, getting together the down payment for a house, how your company could take action to improve the environment, or how to unveil a new project to the public. Whether it is an issue you are actually facing or simply one you selected to exercise your mind, take the issue you pick through a logical progression all the way to a likely end. Most of us can successfully start this type of thinking process. It takes

mental discipline to complete it and not give in to our tendency to stop midway.

2. *Rehash.* Do a postmortem on past issues. Identify what went right and what went wrong. Come up with several possible reasons for both your success in that situation and your mistakes. Rehashing enhances original thinking by helping you avoid making the same mistakes in the future. You also avoid throwing the baby out with the bath water. If something *has* worked for you in the past, there may be no need to replace it with an entirely new approach.

3. *Recognize and reward others' fresh thinking.* Get together with other individuals and share thoughts and ideas related to a particular topic. Brainstorm alternative solutions to problems you have in common. Encourage (or at least don't discourage) "off-the-wall" thinking. The abstract and inconceivable, the odd and initially unimaginable, often lead you in the direction of a workable solution. One idea begets another. Thinking breeds more thinking.

4. *Plant subjects you are considering in the garden of your subconscious.* Put a question or problem into your head before you go to sleep. Tell yourself you need to come up with a new idea. Then stop consciously thinking about it.

5. *Take the alternatives you have and divide them into desirable and undesirable option categories.* You can then divide desirable options into such categories as affordable solutions versus unaffordable solutions, fun versus not fun, productive versus unproductive, and so on. This simple listing of pros and cons is not new. In fact, it seems so elementary that we often fail to use it. Yet it is one of the most practical and effective approaches to decision making.

6. *Think of what would be expected in a given situation. Then think about its opposite.* Use the simple, straightforward approach described at the top of this list to think of the most logical step-by-step way to do things. Then turn your response upside down. (Think, "If I wanted a pay raise, I could. . . ." Then think, "If I wanted a pay raise, I would never. . . ." Or think, "We could unveil a new project by. . . ." Then think, "No one would ever expect us to unveil it by. . . .") By considering those two opposites, you'll often think of an option that falls somewhere in the middle, which will enable you to do what others don't without going to extremes.

7. *Put yourself in someone else's shoes.* Look at the issue from the perspective of other people involved—your employer, employees, competitors, vendors, customers, clients, stockholders, the press, the public, and so on. Taking into account the positions of everyone who holds a stake in the situation helps you clarify your own point of view as well as deal with those who might block you and get additional support from those who are likely to back you.

8. *Play the part of a Monday morning quarterback—but do it on Saturday.* Look at the matter as if it has already been decided and evaluate the "decision." Do this for as many potential outcomes as you can envision. Like someone standing at a window on the top floor of a skyscraper and looking down to get a clearer view of *all* routes into the city, simply play out different scenarios to help you choose the path you'll follow.

9. *Mentally remove constraints.* Create a "best case" outcome by pretending you have no money, time, or personnel limitations. You'll often come up with plans that could work within your constraints—with a few revisions or options for obtaining the resources you need.

10. *Create analogies.* For instance, you might think, "The bickering between those two employees is like a sibling rivalry. They're both vying for 'Daddy's' affection, and they're each jealous of the attention the other one gets." Develop the analogy,

imagining how someone in the situation to which you are comparing your own would handle the problem. (How could the father show both children they are loved and make sure neither one feels neglected?) Then switch back to your issue and ask yourself how you could use comparable methods to resolve it.

11. *Deliberately disrupt logical thought patterns.* Pick out anything in sight and think of how that inanimate object is similar to your situation. You may see an actual connection—for example, "My supervisor's like that window. You can see right through him." But any connection will do—"That apple is as red as my face gets when I'm angry." The point is to sidetrack yourself intentionally so that you can come back to the issue at hand with a fresh perspective.

12. *Have a chat with a "bartender."* Talk to someone who is totally uninvolved in and unconnected to whatever you are pondering. In addition to bartenders, you could discuss the matter with your spouse, taxi drivers, ministers, golfing buddies, hairdressers, or personal fitness trainers. Ask for their ideas, thoughts, and opinions. They'll often provide an entirely new take on matters you are too embroiled in to see clearly.

SHOW YOUR SMARTS—WHEN SPEAKING AND IN WRITING

Competence and smarts won't do you much good if no one knows you have them. Substance without style and presence is largely lost on those you hope to impress. To make it to the top and stay there, you must not only *be* capable, effective, and intelligent, you must *look* as if you are.

Needless to say, style alone is not the answer. Although many would agree with the man who told me, "Looking intelligent helps. It hides a lot," you will find very few "empty suits" (people who have nothing worth mentioning below their highly polished surfaces) at the top of any organization. They don't last.

To succeed in business, you must know your stuff and "strut" it—without going to extremes. You must have the technical expertise and broad-based knowledge to generate ideas and also the personal effectiveness and communication skills to convey your ideas to others.

The higher up you go in an organization, the more important it becomes to express yourself effectively—in person and on paper. You will also be called upon to reach larger and larger audiences—during training seminars, guest speaking engagements, testimonial dinners, and more. If you develop public speaking skills now, you will be able to rise to that challenge throughout your professional life.

> "I believe a good corporate officer should be a good presenter—clear, articulate, and comfortable giving a speech."
>
> —RYAL POPPA
> *Chairman, president, and CEO,*
> *Storage Technology Corporation*

Basic Guidelines for Public Speaking

1. *Adjust your attitude*. The thought of speaking in public inspires great fear and trepidation in many people. They know that if they perform poorly not just one but dozens (or hundreds) of people are going to see them. They are afraid that they will embarrass themselves and that the embarrassment they feel will be multiplied by the number of people in the room, thus making it unbearable. Their fear becomes a self-fulfilling prophecy when anxiety prompts them to make mistakes and turn in the poor performance they had dreaded all along. By adjusting your attitude ahead of time, you can avoid the same fate.

If you can hold your own in a one-on-one conversation, you can teach yourself to feel comfortable in front of an audience. When speaking to fifty people, simply think of yourself as conducting fifty one-on-one conversations. The only difference is that you are having those conversations simultaneously. Each audience member is listening, interpreting, disagreeing, or agreeing with you on a one-to-one basis. So tell yourself, "I'm not talking to a group of fifty. I am having fifty personal conversations at once!"

2. *Be prepared. Talk about what you know well.* (Sometimes you might be called upon to speak extemporaneously or to expound on subjects only remotely related to your area of expertise. If you have advance notice, you can research the topic. If you don't, do your best to address the topic and then steer yourself back onto more familiar ground.)

When preparing a speech, follow the basic outline taught in most high school English classes:

- tell them what you're going to tell them;
- tell them;
- tell them what you told them.

Organize the "tell them" section so that you:

- make a point or state an opinion;
- then elaborate on your point by using an illustration, story, or anecdote;
- then give the reasoning behind your point or opinion;
- and finally restate your point or opinion.

Or you can plan to:

- make a point or state an opinion;
- then elaborate on your point with an illustration, story, or anecdote;
- then ask a question in order to involve the audience or your fellow panel members and get their reactions to the point(s) you made (by asking questions, you take the pressure off yourself, keep from rambling on too long, and give yourself a moment to think about the next point you'll make);

- then recapture the audience's attention with a second story or illustration;
- and finally, restate your initial point or position.

3. *If your schedule permits, spend time with your audience in advance.* Go up to them, introduce yourself, shake hands, read their name tags, and make small talk to show humanness and get personal. When they've touched and conversed with you, shared a laugh or two, and had personal contact with you, the members of your audience feel that they know you. As a result, during your presentation you'll receive a more favorable response from them.

4. *After you are introduced, get to the lectern in a deliberate, enthusiastic manner.* Walk slowly and purposefully—but not lethargically. Pause when you reach the lectern, look at the audience, and pause again. Only after you have their complete attention should you start to speak.

5. *Stand erect with both feet firmly planted on the stage or platform.* Don't lean against a chair, lectern, or wall. You'll give a too casual or laissez-faire impression (or just plain look lazy and tired). Toe tapping and other nervous foot movements make you look insecure, and the audience will begin to doubt what you are saying. Be especially careful about this when you're standing on a stage with your feet at the audience's eye level.

6. *Make eye contact with individual members of the audience.* Many speakers scan the audience as they speak, letting their gaze stop on individual members of the audience for less than a second before moving on to the next. Their goal—to make everyone feel included—is a worthy one. But constant side-to-side movement of their eyes and heads makes them look nervous and skittish to the people who are watching them. Instead, do what you would do if you were talking one-on-one—make sustained eye contact with people. Look at an individual face and keep your eyes on that person for as long as it takes you to complete your comment or thought. Then after a good five to ten seconds, you can select another person and direct your gaze at him or her—again maintaining visual contact for the time it takes you to convey an entire thought. Although your natural inclination will be to keep coming back to the friendliest faces, try to look at nonplussed or even seemingly unfriendly ones as well.

7. *Use gestures to help make your points with the audience and to make your presentation more enjoyable.* You will be viewed as a more dynamic, informed, and interesting speaker if you use purposeful movement along with your verbal presentation. Match the size of your gesture to the size of the audience, using broader gestures for large groups and subtler ones (like those you'd rely on in a one-to-one conversation) for smaller groups.

8. *Use humor during your presentation.* That does not mean starting out with "A funny thing happened on the way . . ." or "Did you hear the one about . . . ?" Instead, use the suggestions found in chapter 15 to inject humor that relates to the subject matter of your speech and is appropriate for the occasion. It will help you bond with your audience and keep them interested in what you have to say.

Additional Tips

1. *If you have advance notice and the time to do it, prepare a script.* Turning the paper lengthwise, draw a line down the middle of each page and type your speech (or a detailed outline) on one side. Then on the other side sketch pictures that correspond to and illustrate your points. You'll find that it's much easier to follow your outline by quickly glancing at your sketches than by trying to read the shrinking print. In addition, your illustrated script will help your presentation flow more smoothly by creating a bridge from one idea to another. It's particularly beneficial for getting you back on track if you lose your place (or get detoured by questions from the audience).

2. *If possible, give your speech before you give your speech.* Prior to presenting a talk to your audience, you might give it to your dinner companions, your jogging buddies, friends, colleagues, or fellow conference participants. Try out your jokes. Make some of the points you plan to make later. Gauge their reactions. By rehearsing in this manner, you get to do last-minute fine-tuning and get a feel for your audience's probable response. Let them know what you're doing. They usually won't mind and may feel honored to be part of your inner circle and a confidant whose opinion you obviously value.

3. *Try not to hide behind the lectern.* The more people can see of you, the more attention they will pay to you. Your notes will still be there if you need to consult them, and most microphones are made to be mobile. So get out from behind the lectern. Don't use it as a crutch.

4. *If possible, remove your eyeglasses.* They glare in the lights, preventing others from "looking you in the eye." Many people who are extremely near-sighted purposely remove their eyeglasses so that they can't see the members of the audience clearly and, consequently, feel less intimidated by them.

5. *Beware of "reading" too much into audience members' body language.* You are likely to be wrong.

Not long ago I was giving a speech, and every time I made a key point, a man in the second row shook his head as one would when saying "no." After a while, it became quite distracting. So I called a break and casually went over to him to ask if he was simply disagreeing or if he felt my points weren't well argued. "Oh, no!" he said. "I'm shaking my head because I can't believe how many times I've done these things incorrectly."

On another occasion, a man in the audience caught my attention because every time I looked in his direction, he was nodding his head up and down as if enthusiastically agreeing with me. It was great positive reinforcement for me as a lecturer, and during the break, I made a point of thanking him for his support. Again he nodded in what I assumed to be appreciation, but did not say much. Later I would learn from others that he had Parkinson's disease and his nodding was a symptom of his illness—not a reflection of my brilliance.

In both instances, I misinterpreted the behavior I observed from the podium. Although no great harm was done, I did unnecessarily clutter my mind with guesses as to how I was being received. I urge you not to make the same mistake. Remember that you will always be more professional as a speaker than the people to whom you are speaking are professional as an audience. They seldom know how to make you feel comfortable. You need to pay attention to the audience's reaction without reading too much into it.

6. *If you intend using charts, overhead projections, or other audiovisual aids, rehearse with them beforehand.* If you find that you look clumsy while using them, it's better not to use them at all. Instead enhance your performance with your own audiovisual effects—movement, facial expressions, and voice.

The proper sequence for using a flip chart is:

- with your hand or a pointer, draw attention to a specific point;
- select one member of the audience to look at and talk to while making that point;
- *then* speak;
- repeat the same sequence for each point.

Do *not* talk while flipping the sheet, fixing the sheet, or looking at the chart.

7. *Make sure that you hold a transparency or product and receive or present a plaque "specially."* If you watch airline attendants when flight safety instructions are being given, you'll notice that they hold the instruction card, oxygen mask, and other demonstration materials like pieces of art being auctioned at Christie's. Why? Because it draws attention to those items and conveys their importance.

According to Tom Henrion, president of KFC National Purchasing Cooperative, Inc., counter clerks are taught to "present" trays of food to customers with both hands and with respect. Doing so leaves others with a more favorable impression of the clerk and the fast-food chain. The same principle applies to anything you hold while speaking in public. Whether it is a piece of paper, a workbook, contract, product, pointer, plaque, or trophy, if you want to let your audience know that what you are holding is important as well as gain their attention and respect, handle the item purposefully, with importance and care.

8. *If you are part of a panel, remember that you are on-stage all the time—not just when you are speaking.* Control your posture, facial expression, and movements. Watch and listen to the other panelists, nodding or shaking your head in agreement or disagreement. You will make a very definite point, because even though you aren't speaking, the audience is watching you.

Effectively Handling Questions and Answers

1. *When you are ready to take questions, let the audience know verbally AND nonverbally.* Say, "Any questions?" and raise your own hand to let individuals in your audience know how you want them to indicate that they have questions. People will usually mirror what they see. If you raise your hand, they are more likely to raise theirs.

2. *Before giving your answer, restate (and if necessary rephrase) the question.* Restating enables the entire audience to hear the question and helps you plan your answer to it. By rephrasing, you can get the question to address the issue as you prefer it to be addressed. For instance, if asked, "Will you explain your late delivery of the product?" you might restate it to say, "The question was about the timeliness of our deliveries."

3. *After someone asks a question do not say "good question."* If you say that to everyone, you sound insincere. If you say it to some and not others, the people who have asked questions without receiving a positive comment about their question feel that their question wasn't good. Likewise *do not refer to the person asking the question by name unless you can (and plan to) call everyone in the audience by name.* When you refer to some people by name but not others you appear to be "playing favorites," and anyone who doesn't get called by name feels left out of your "little clique."

4. *When answering one person's question, make eye contact with someone else.* Why? Because looking at the person who asked the question while you answer it increases the odds that:

- Should your answer fail to satisfy that person, you'll try harder to explain yourself to him or her and ultimately lose control over the interaction. In public speaking, making eye contact with the person who asks the question says "I accept your challenge" and invites him to challenge you further.
- The rest of the audience will feel excluded. Whenever you allow yourself to be drawn into a dialogue with one audience member, you run the risk of losing your rapport with the audience as a whole.

Making eye contact with someone other than the person who asks the question is difficult to do—especially when someone is trying to "nail you to the wall." Set a precedent (and get some practice) by controlling your eye contact when answering relatively easy questions. That will make it easier for you to use the same technique with the tough questions as well.

5. *Do not check with people to find out if your answer satisfied them.* Maintain your position as the authority, answer the question to the best of your ability, and then move on.

6. *Try to answer at least one question with a one-word answer.* ("Yes," "No," "Two," "None," etc.) It keeps you from looking wordy and gives you instant credibility. It is also unexpected, so much so that audiences often respond to one-word answers with laughter or applause and you build rapport.

7. *Whether you are stymied or simply want to encourage audience participation, you always have the option of referring questions back to your audience.* You might ask, "Can anyone answer that?" or "Do any of you who have experienced similar problems have any insights to offer this gentleman?"

USE SMARTS TO MAKE YOUR CORRESPONDENCE CONVEY YOUR COMPETENCE

In this age of instant communication via telephone, computer, or fax machine, the value and impact of well-written correspondence is often overlooked. However, writing to people in your own hand on high-quality paper is an excellent way to make a favorable impression, bond, and set yourself apart from the crowd. Do what others don't—write. Write frequently. Write to thank, notify, request, praise, correct, inquire, and more. And write smart.

Most of us receive far more correspondence than we can handle thoroughly, and it increases ten-fold at each succeeding rung of the corporate ladder. Consequently, when writing to anyone and especially when writing to any senior executive, you must make sure that your correspondence stands out, instantly captures the reader's attention, and effectively gets your message across. In person, you only have a few seconds or at most a few minutes to make a favorable first impression. In writing, you have even less time than that.

How to Write Smart

1. *Know your purpose. Be succinct. Don't BS.* People who don't know what they want to say (or are afraid to say it) ramble

and beat around the bush. The people who receive their correspondence know that and tend to think of the correspondent as wordy, unsure of himself, and amateurish. (After all, a competent professional would know that other professionals don't want to waste their time reading lengthy letters filled with extraneous details.) Although it takes longer to write a short, succinct letter than a long, rambling one, take the time. You make a favorable impression (and improve the odds that your letter will get read) when you get to your point quickly and make your point with the fewest possible words.

I learned how effective a very brief, very succinct letter can be from Mike Wilfley, president of A. R. Wilfley & Sons, Inc. He replied to one of my standard inquiry letters neatly typed on company stationery by returning my own letter to me with the following note attached:

> *Dear Debra,*
>
> > *Yes.*
> > *No.*
> > *Maybe.*
> > *Good Idea.*
>
> *Regards,*
> *Mike*

In five words, he effectively and efficiently addressed, point by point, the lengthy questions found in my original letter.

2. *Use the following simple but effective letter outline.*

A. Make the first paragraph *reader oriented*. Address the other person directly and capture his attention with a compliment or comment that "hits his hot button." Start with "you" not "I." "You seem to be the person I need to talk to." "Your company is known as a leader in. . . ." "You did a terrific job on. . . ."

B. Make the second paragraph *writer oriented*. Tell the reader why you are writing. "I'm interested in. . . ." "I want to. . . ." "I'd like. . . ."

C. Make the third paragraph an *action* paragraph. Inform the reader of the next action you will take. "We need to. . . ." "I'll call you next week to. . . ." "I'll send the. . . ." "You and I could. . . ."

If you need to communicate complex or extensive information in your letter, stick to the outline but expand the letter by including additional paragraphs in part B. To convey a great deal of information, write a cover letter and keep it brief. Then enclose additional information in report form.

I used that approach when I was writing to the top people I hoped to interview for this book. Combining part A and part B of the foregoing outline into one sentence and requesting action in a second sentence, I sent out the following two paragraph note handwritten on Crane card stock:

Dear _____,

You would be interesting to talk with for a book I'm writing on traits at the top.

Could we schedule an interview sometime during (month)?

Debra Benton

I attached the note to my company brochure (to show that I was a real person). As you can see from the long list of names in the acknowledgments, my effort to address the reader briefly and succinctly, explain my purpose, and request action was successful.

3. *Keep each paragraph short.* If you can make your point in one or two sentences per paragraph, all the better.

4. *Talk to the reader in writing.* Use the same words you'd use if you were speaking to him or her in person. You'll be more likely to deal with a person human-to-human rather than role-to-role. The former is always more interesting (and unexpected) than the latter.

HOW TO STAY SMART—AND GET SMARTER

"To really succeed, you need to persevere through the ups and the downs. You must also be willing to continue your education so that you always know what's going on in the world."

—LAWRENCE WEINBACH
Managing partner-CEO, Arthur Andersen and Co.

Chiefs stay smart and get smarter every day. You can too if you:

1. *Keep abreast of current events.* Read newspapers, listen to the radio, and watch television.

2. *Keep an eye on current trends.* Read *Forbes*, *Fortune*, the *Wall Street Journal*, *Business Week*, *Investors Weekly*, *Newsweek*, *Time*, and so on. While reading:

- think about how the information applies to you and your business;
- plan ways to use the information in the future;
- go back and review plans you've made previously and, as needed, revise them to reflect or address the new information you've obtained.

3. *Keep up with changes in technology.* Make sure you have access to information about research being conducted in your field. You might want to hire a clipping service that can constantly supply you with the latest information about your industry.

4. *Be well connected personally.* Through business relation-ships you may be able to receive information before it reaches the media or the public. Keep an up-to-date list of sources from whom you can get "scoops." Do not rely solely on subordinates whose information is apt to be geared toward what they think you want to hear (which may not be what you actually need to know). Instead, make a list of people with whom it would be beneficial to spend time and deliberately go about meeting those people. Develop personal connections with them and don't be afraid to use your connections to obtain the information you need.

Finally, to continue to develop more smarts and use them effectively, be sure to:

- think creatively;
- encourage creative thinking in others;
- look for fresh, innovative perspectives and communicate what you've learned;
- set aside time to develop new thought patterns and practice using them. You'll form a positive habit and feel motivated to come up with even more fresh, innovative, and effective ideas.

21

Lucky Breaks—
See Your Chance, Take It,
and Make It to the Top

"The people who make it to the top have luck. They
have drive, curiosity, flexibility, and thoroughness. But
they also have luck."

—LOUIS MATTIS
Chairman and CEO, Sterling Drug Inc.

The other chiefs I interviewed wholeheartedly agreed with
that statement. In fact, most of them claimed that their own
success was largely due to luck—and they weren't just being
modest. Although one CEO did say, "Because I'm good at what
I do, I believe I'd be here today no matter what," most insisted
that they had simply "been at the right place at the right time."

Of course, they *had* worked hard to get there. A combination
of optimism, courage, smarts, and steady, persistent effort got
them to the right place. Then they trusted their instincts and
took the right action at the right time.

"A key turning point in my career—and a lucky one—
came when I was twenty-four and working at Vicks'. I
picked NyQuil out of a pile of trashed projects and

worked night and day to sell it to management. I don't know what made me pick it, but it obviously turned out well."

—**MICHAEL LESSER**
President, Ogilvy & Mather

Top people will say that they *got* lucky breaks. However, like Lesser, they actually *made* most of their own luck. You can too.

YOU CAN'T CONTROL EVERYTHING

Naturally, there are some variables that simply are beyond human control, and whether you call them flukes, twists of fate, or karma, they have been known to influence the outcome of countless situations. Something as completely uncontrollable as your parentage (and whether or not your family encouraged you to achieve or could afford to pay for a top-notch education) can give you a head start in the business world or create obstacles for you to overcome. So can:

- your race, color, creed, sex, or height;
- the right or wrong business cycle;
- good or bad bosses;
- good or bad companies;
- good or bad marriages;
- good or bad health.

Unfair as it may be, because of these and other "circumstances beyond your control," you may have more or fewer opportunities to succeed than other people. But that doesn't mean you can wait for lucky breaks, depend on luck to pull you through situations that you have not adequately prepared yourself to handle, or blame bad luck, weak genes, or the configuration of the planets when you fail.

Whether you were born with a silver spoon in your mouth or

were a poor coal miner's daughter, went to Harvard or worked your way through a state university, have the best boss in the world or the worst, you can still take charge of the things within your control (most notably your behavior and its effect) and take full advantage of every opportunity that does present itself. When you do, you'll become luckier, and everything you do to become luckier will contribute to your short-term and long-term success.

YOU ARE AS LUCKY AS YOU THINK YOU ARE

While serving in Korea, J. Richard Munro, cochairman and co-CEO of Time Warner, Inc., was badly wounded. Some might call that bad luck. Munro didn't. He described the incident this way, "It was pitch dark, but I heard the grenade land beside me and roll past my head to my feet before going off and throwing me twenty feet in the air. It had blown my legs all to hell, but it could have stopped at my head and blown that up. I've had that sort of good fortune all of my life."

To hear Munro tell it, his entire career involved one stroke of luck after another. "Another time, after being number-two man at *Sports Illustrated*, I was sent to Chicago to run some newspapers. Two months later, the publisher of *Sports Illustrated* was promoted to head up *Life* magazine and there was a meeting to choose his replacement. I was the likely candidate, but one man said, 'We just moved him to Chicago two months ago. We can't bring him back to New York so soon.' My old boss asked, 'Why the hell not?' and I was back in the running. Now if it hadn't been for luck, my old boss would have been in the men's room, never have made that comment, and I wouldn't have gotten the job."

Was becoming the publisher of *Sports Illustrated* really a matter of luck? Or did Munro get the job because he was the best candidate for it? We'll never know for sure. But the more important point is that Munro thought of himself as "lucky enough to be successful"—and he was. He expected factors he had no control over to "break" in his favor—and they did. He looked for signs of his good fortune—and found them. His *attitude* improved his luck—and yours can too.

We *all* have both good luck and bad luck. If we dwell on our misfortune, mulling over our bad breaks and unfavorably comparing ourselves to people who seem to "have all the luck," we undermine our self-confidence, talk ourselves out of taking risks that could advance our careers, and as a result, stop short of our goals. Conversely, if we think about our good fortune, remind ourselves of the lucky breaks we've had over the years, and tell ourselves that we have every reason to expect good luck in the future, we feel more self-confident. We take more risks. We experience more success. And we get luckier.

You will be as lucky as you think you are, as lucky as you feel, and as lucky as your overall attitude allows you to be. So you are wise to adopt the attitude that the late Norman Cousins conveyed when he said, "I've been relentlessly pursued by luck all my life."

As the saying goes, "luck is what happens when preparation meets opportunity."

> "You have to move though the chairs and serve your time. But you also need to be aware of opportunities to break away from the pack. My big break was making a presentation on the results of a study that triggered the frequent flyer industry. It was a combination of awareness, personal exposure, and my decision to latch on to that particular project."
>
> —THOMAS G. PLASKETT
> *Chairman, president, and CEO,*
> *Pan-American Corporation*

Opportunities to make a favorable impression, establish bonds, create a niche for yourself, or break out of a rut and make a name for yourself are infinite in number and varied in nature. On any given day you may have the opportunity to:

- strike up a conversation with someone who could advance your career;
- propose an innovative solution to a long-standing problem;
- read about a technique that could save your company time and money;
- volunteer for a project that could get your picture in the newspaper;
- follow up on an idea that popped into your head while you were driving to work or taking a shower;
- and much more.

You have to look for those opportunities and "mine" them for all they're worth. You make your own luck by learning to recognize an opportunity to stand out, fit in, or get ahead when you see one and *being prepared* to take advantage of that opportunity when it arises.

How do you prepare to be lucky? By "doing the legwork"—developing competence, confidence, areas of expertise, people skills, the willingness to initiate, and the courage to do what others don't. Plenty of people will get the same opportunities you do. You have to be the one with the guts to grasp them, the one who won't allow a fear of failure to prevent you from trying to succeed and the one who is *willing to put in the effort in order to reap the rewards*.

LUCK IS THE RESIDUE OF HARD WORK

"I was teaching an 'alternative' college course on internal politics—on how to handle a job once you have it—and a reporter wrote an article about me. A book publisher who saw the article called to ask if I'd write a book on the subject I was teaching. I said, 'I don't write unless someone pays me.' She said, 'Write an

outline.' I did, and the next thing I knew, I had a contract, then a best-selling book."
—**BETTY LEHAN HARRAGAN**
Author, Games Mother Never Taught You

Maybe no one has ever asked *you* to write a book. Maybe no one ever will. But lucky breaks in one form or another are available to everyone. Whether or not you "cash in" on the luck that comes your way is entirely up to you.

During one of my conversations with Ernie Howell, retired president of St. Regis/WPM, he said, "The object in life is first to recognize opportunities and second to *act on them.* You'll always be lucky if you keep taking chances. The unlucky don't grasp opportunities. The lucky do. It's that simple."

Then he proceeded to quote verbatim the following passage from Shakespeare's *Julius Caesar:* " 'There is a tide in the affairs of men, which, taken at the flood, leads on to fortune; omitted, all the voyage of their life is bound in shallows and in miseries. On such a full sea are we now afloat; and we must take the current when it serves, or lose our ventures.'

"When that flood tide comes," he advised, "Get in the boat and go or else you'll be stuck in the backwaters of life forever."

All of us would do well to take that advice—and take action to make the most of the lucky breaks we get. Opportunities don't do us much good unless we do something with them. In addition, what we do and especially the application of effort over time often creates situations in which luck will come our way.

Despite a "shoestring budget," a consultant to charitable organizations had managed to line up all of the donated goods and services she needed to produce a television public service announcement. Unfortunately, the individual who had promised to get a sports personality to appear in the spot let her down. She was "frantically rewriting the commercial" when she learned that a nationally known hockey player would be speaking at her nephew's hockey banquet. "With only two weeks to go before the event where I planned to unveil the commercial, I was willing to try anything," she said. "So I got a bunch of materials together, took them to the hockey banquet, and after that player was finished speaking, I marched right up to him and asked him to bail me out. He took my card and the materials I'd brought along to prove that I was legit and called me the next day to say he'd do it." He also said he decided to do it because he saw how much work she had put into the project and didn't think it should go to waste.

To be lucky you must be active. You can't wait for things to happen. You have to go out and make them happen. Work hard. Plan ahead. Initiate. Exert control over the variables that are within your control and you'll improve the odds that the uncontrollable variables will work in your favor. And if they don't? Use the very same principles and practices to make the best of a bad situation.

THE WORST OF LUCK—GETTING FIRED

As far as most businesspeople are concerned, the ultimate bad-luck situation (and the one they fear most) is being out of a job. Getting fired, released, laid off, retired early, phased out, outplaced, or whatever else a company wants to call it not only leaves people without steady paychecks and something productive to do for eight or more hours a day. It also deals a powerful blow to their self-confidence and all too often is perceived as a permanent black mark on their record, a failure that forever after will limit their chances to succeed. But that need not be the case.

As you may recall, early in my career, I got fired. The person who terminated me said I was honest, competent, and hard-working but unproductive because I didn't deal with many different types of people effectively. Although I was mortified and felt like a complete failure at the time, encountering that harsh and decidedly unpleasant reality also woke me up, slapped me across the face, and motivated me to change.

I had lost my job because I lacked something I knew virtually nothing about—people skills—and I decided to find out as much about them as I could. After all, I didn't want to put myself in a position to be fired again. I wanted to learn from my mistakes and figure out how people who had satisfying personal and successful professional lives got them so that I could too. That became the driving force for my research on what it takes to get to the top. Years later when the president of a college would ask me, "What made you so dedicated and committed?" My answer was, "Being fired."

As it did for me, losing your job can turn out well *if you learn from it.* First and foremost, learn why you lost that job. Then learn what you can do to keep yourself out of similar situations in the future, and then follow through.

The Most Common Reasons for Being Fired

1. *You weren't performing and didn't deserve the paycheck.* (You can develop more competence by increasing your knowledge and skill and improving your work habits. Then put in more effort next time.)

2. *You were performing so well that you were a threat to someone who had the power to fire you.* (Although this might fall under the heading of "circumstances beyond your control," you could try taking a closer look at prospective bosses while you are job hunting or developing additional people skills and using them to establish positive relationships with people you think could be threatened by your competence. In your next job, learn the politics of the organization and how to "work" them.)

3. *Your "chemistry" wasn't right for that particular organization. You didn't "fit in."* (Again, being choosy and developing people skills are the answer. You can fit in almost anywhere if you learn how to bond.)

4. *You got caught in a merger or acquisition. New management came in and "swept the place clean."* (Just plain bad luck. Pick yourself up, dust yourself off, and get back in the running.)

5. *You were dishonest.* Every top person asked felt justified in firing an employee for dishonesty. If you are going to lie, cheat, or steal, you can't expect to get away with it forever—and you don't deserve to get ahead in business. So, just don't do any of those things.

Learn from your experiences or you'll run the risk of repeating them. Being fired several times *is* a problem, and being fired several times for the same reason can be seriously detrimental to your career.

Although you may think you don't need the foregoing advice, my experience as a consultant to many different companies has taught me that *no job is totally secure.* In fact, most jobs rest on the shakiest of foundations—the unpredictable and constantly changing emotions of immediate supervisors, boards of directors, or customer bases. Up and down the corporate ladder, people have lost their supposedly secure jobs literally overnight. Even so, you can't live in fear of being terminated. If you do, you'll never find the courage to do what it takes to get ahead in the business world. Instead, *always have a Plan B.*

Years ago, I saw an old movie about an Australian who was trying to build a life for himself in the United States. Because he came from a landed family, he had a "Plan B"—he could always return to work on the family ranch. Consequently, each time he had a difficult choice to make or encountered a situation in which he could fail, he'd say, "Well, there's always Australia," and make the choice or take the risk. His Plan B gave him a feeling of security that allowed him to forge ahead and do what was required for success.

Whether it involves going back to school full time, starting your own business, taking a year off to travel, or getting back in touch with the headhunter who called you last month, your Plan B can do the same for you. You might even find it helpful to keep an undated, unsigned resignation letter in your desk. It could be as simple as:

Dear _____,

   As of this date I resign from my position at XYZ. I wish you and XYZ all the best for the future.

Sincerely,

Of course, actually using your Plan B has ramifications. For instance, if you resign rather than get released, it could severely affect the financial separation package the company would offer you. However, simply by knowing and reminding yourself that you have other options, you reduce your fear of termination and can make better decisions—including those that will ensure that you don't have to use your Plan B.

If you do have the misfortune to get fired, exert as much control over the situation as you can. Companies and the individuals in them are notorious for handling terminations poorly. As perverse as it sounds, if you want the firing to be done effectively, you have to take charge. When you do, you're more likely to walk away with your dignity and sense of self-worth intact— unlike the bank president who sadly told me, "One day I was on top of my profession. The next day I was fired. The third day I totally lost my self-esteem."

What to Do If You Are Fired

1. *Maintain your presence.*

- Listen carefully to exactly what is being said. Don't interrupt. Listen.
- If possible, write down what's being said.
- Don't bother trying to get the person who is terminating you to explain or defend his position. Assume the decision that has been made is final and . . .
- Don't try to change the other person's mind. It's wasted effort.
- Don't cry. You'll only embarrass yourself and others.

2. *Ask questions.* After the other person has finished talking, pause, compose yourself, and then ask questions. Sit there a minute, breathe deeply, look out the window, relax yourself, and ask:

- "When does this take effect?" Find out the exact date they want you to stop working, clean out your desk, and return the office keys.
- "What is the financial separation package you're proposing?" Learn what they plan to offer. Ask about severance pay, vacation and sick pay, insurance continuance (who will be paying for it and how long will it be available), use of the office, telephone, copy machine, and so on, use of secretarial services (typing, telephone messages, etc.), and outplacement services.

You need to know these things and you have nothing to lose by asking. (What are they going to do, fire you?)

3. *Speak up for yourself. You have the option to ask for more.* They can only say "yes" or "no." Too many people just accept what's offered. You may be surprised by what is available—if you ask.

After hearing their offer, make a statement acknowledging the dismissal and asking for time to think about the separation package. I suggest you say something like "I realize this must be difficult for you to do. It's obviously a blow to me. I understand what you've told me, and I need time to think about it. I'm not going to try to change your mind, but I'm sure I will have more questions. I'd like to discuss the separation agreement further in a day or two."

When the separation package is settled, request a written agreement. Don't leave your future to someone else's selective memory. Get the terms of your separation in writing.

4. *Hang in there. Don't tell the other person exactly what you think of him, the way he handled the dismissal, or the decision* *to dismiss you.* Saying, "You SOB, I've never liked you. In fact, you're the worst boss I ever had," may feel great at that moment; but it's detrimental in the long run. Although it's easier said than done, try not to burn your bridges behind you. It's not inconceivable that at some point in the future the person who fired you could be in the position to rehire you. Joseph V. Vittoria headed up Avis Europe, lost his position, joined Hertz, and then was asked to rejoin Avis as chairman and CEO.

Go home—not to a bar. Give yourself the afternoon off. Gather the family and explain the situation. Your spouse, children, and maybe even parents have part of their identities linked to your career. Their reaction will be a reflection of your own. If you keep your attitude of good cheer, they will too. If you feel defeated, they will also. Try to inject some humor into the conversation—and be willing to accept their comfort and support.

Finally, keep in mind that no matter how bleak things seem at the moment, getting fired may have given you a great opportunity. At the very least, you are freed from a significant restriction in making a major change. In many instances, the next job you get or the new direction you take will bring you closer to achieving your goals. As Warren McCain, chairman and CEO of Albertson's, puts it, "You don't always win. Take the weekend and feel sorry for yourself. Then go out and show the bastards their mistake."

LUCK TURNS

"I grew up in the corporate mold with a lot of my self-worth tied up in my career and a great fear of losing the corporate security blanket. Then, the company I worked for was acquired, and I was asked to take a job without the scope and responsibility of the one I'd held previously. Although I wasn't terminated, I felt as if I had been. But I didn't die and I realized I wasn't going

to lose my spouse, my children, or my home because
I was losing my old job. That was a critical turning
point for me. It gave me inner confidence, a greater
appetite for risk and accomplishment rather than career
orientation."

—**LOUIS MATTIS**
Chairman and CEO, Sterling Drug Inc.

As this extremely successful individual discovered, a bit of bad
luck (and even a run of it) isn't deadly. What's more, it doesn't
last. Life runs in cycles. Good luck turns bad. Bad luck turns
good. And sometimes bad luck is lucky because it throws you
into a situation you might not have chosen for yourself, but once
there, you are successful.

"My good luck is what I use to extricate myself from
my bad luck."

—**JIM RUPP**
Attorney

"A secret of my success is recognizing when my good luck is
turning bad and getting out of that situation," says David Lam,
who manages forty companies worldwide. Obviously, his approach works. At one time he controlled 70 percent of the world's
rice and has been recognized as one of the top businesspeople
in Hong Kong.

No matter what is happening at any given moment, remember
that both good and bad luck come and go. When you get a lucky
break, take advantage of it. When things start to sour or bad luck
strikes, take action to cut your losses and move on. With thought,
guts, and effort, you'll turn things around, and your bad luck
will change to good luck again. The application of effort over
time *always* wins out—and that's where your real luck comes
from.

22

Life at the Top

What is it *really* like at the top? "More complex than I thought it would be," said Ronald Unkefer, chairman and CEO of the Good Guys. "Sometimes I feel as uncertain as I did when I started."

"The demands become greater," Rose Marie Bravo, president of I. Magnin, Inc., explained. "There's no such thing as 'now I've made it' and I can relax. There is increasing work load, stress, and responsibility."

According to Tom Freston, president and CEO of MTV Networks, "You never feel that you *are* at the top."

Larry Colin, president of Colin Service Systems, Inc., agreed. "You need to perform continuously in order to continuously remind yourself that you're not an imposter."

Bill Morin, chairman of Drake, Beam, Morin, added, "Success to me is actually causing a ripple in life. I feel I've contributed, not necessarily succeeded."

Other chiefs described life at the top as follows:

> "Sometimes the journey seems endless. You're going to the top of the hill and you've gone through the

water obstacles, through the bushes, dealt with the boogeyman behind the trees. Then, once you're at the top, you notice another mountain range that you hadn't seen before. And somehow the mountain you just climbed doesn't look very high anymore."

—**JOHN BIANCHI**
Chairman, Bianchi International

"At lower levels, your actions have a lot of effect even though you don't have power. At higher levels you have lots of power but you also have: 1. more constituencies to deal with; 2. many people who need to be handled differently; 3. the need to be more circumspect in how you handle your power."

—**ROGER WERNER**
President and CEO, Primesports Ventures

"As an entrepreneur, I had a concept and a vision of the business, but I didn't realize the details involved. It's much more fun to get to the top than be at the top, I can assure you."

—**DAVE LINIGER**
CEO, RE/MAX International

As you can see, being at the top is not exactly the nirvana we imagine it to be when we're clinging to the lower rungs of the corporate ladder. But that doesn't mean top people don't want to be where they are or that they resent having to work hard to stay there. They thrive on the challenges of leadership. They welcome new opportunities to prove themselves. They chose their path and stuck with it for the rewards of the journey and not just to reach a specific destination. In fact, once successful people achieve one level of success, they invariably seek another.

People who expect to get to certain positions of authority and then rest on their laurels, or make their fortunes by age thirty and then retire to a tropical island, rarely make it to the top. As John M. Richards, president and COO of Potlatch Corporation, said, "You can't just be the boss and ride that for the next ten or fifteen years."

At the top, you have to work just as hard as you did on the way up and sometimes even harder than you ever worked in your entire life. More than anyone else, chiefs heed the advice to "work hard and listen." They listen to find out what to work on and then work hard on that.

WHAT CHANGES WHEN YOU GET TO THE TOP

"I can't forget I'm chairman. It's not Lod Cook calling, it's the chairman. I have to be careful about what I say and how I say things."

—LODWRICK COOK
Chairman and CEO, ARCO

The stakes are higher at the top. An error can cost millions of dollars instead of thousands. Instead of listening to one boss, you may have to answer to ten members of the board of directors. And to complicate matters further, you have to obtain information from and delegate to many levels of management.

"The president isn't as in touch as I thought. The lines of communication and authority prevent information from flowing upward."

—ROBERT DILENSCHNEIDER
President and CEO, Hill and Knowlton, Inc.

"It's surprising how carefully I have to watch how I joke. Saying something like 'Seattle is nice, maybe I'll move the headquarters there,' gets everybody worried."

—ALEX MANDL
Chairman and CEO, Sea Land Service, Inc.

"You don't have the freedom you thought you'd have.
You can't say things in jest anymore."

—**THOMAS BICKETT**
President and COO, Witco Corporation

At the top, you have more freedom to make decisions, to make mistakes, to initiate, to be human, and to use humor. But you have less freedom to say or do whatever comes to mind. Even casual comments carry weight. Your subordinates watch you very carefully and often believe that anything you say is "the law." Consequently, when you get to the top, you'll have to use your smarts and choose your words carefully, constantly considering the effect they may have on others. One chief's advice on this subject is, "Always take a few seconds to say to yourself what you're going to say out loud and prethink others' reactions." You also must take into consideration the mystique that surrounds successful people and affects other people's reactions to you.

Once you get to the top, you may be the same person, but others will perceive you differently. People who were once your peers but who are now your subordinates lose sight of the person they used to joke with freely or pour their hearts out to. They see you as your role. They put you on a pedestal and alternately treat you like an all-knowing God or look for flaws and signs that you are about to fall out of power. This is particularly problematic when you'd prefer to keep a low profile so you can learn what others are really doing and thinking.

Your being the center of attention and constantly being looked upon as the "head honcho" with the power to make or break others' careers biases people and their behavior toward you. You don't want your subordinates to "play up" to you. You need them to relax and open up to you. Your success and the future of your organization depend on their response to your leadership.

"My self-esteem is enhanced by doing my job well.
Therefore, I want the best resources available to me.
One of those resources is people. The fact is, I am

more effective if my people are more effective, but the people who work for me may not be aware that I feel that way. I'm always surprised by the power my subordinates assume I have over them. I'm relatively unconscious of this power. I am more likely to see them as having power over me. Their power lies in the fact that, for many reasons, they can fail to execute plans effectively. 'Bossdom is in the eye of the beholder.' "

—CURT CARTER
Chairman, Mission Bay Investments, Inc.

"There is a general feeling of powerlessness at the top. I'm still subject to the need to coax, persuade, manage, and even manipulate. I found I couldn't command anything just because of my position. The persuasive powers you need to get to the top are still needed once you're there."

—RUSSEL BANKS
President, Grow Group, Inc.

The power that both Carter and Banks are referring to is not necessarily power over others but rather the personal power to change the corporation and to move the company in a positive, profitable direction. No matter how high up the corporate ladder you go, you truly are powerless if your subordinates won't follow your lead. That is why people skills are so crucial at the top. With them, you motivate, build confidence, enhance self-esteem, create a sense of belonging, encourage cooperation, and establish the personal bonds that enable you to lead effectively. Without them, your position, title, and authority are useless. Unless you use your people skills, your people won't produce. If your people don't produce, you'll lose your job. You will no doubt be acutely aware of that fact. At the top you'll worry more and have more to worry about.

"If anyone were to describe my management style they'd say I was laid back. But the truth is I'm really paranoid that things aren't going to work. I worry all the time."

—**ALVAR GREEN**
Chairman, president, and CEO, Autodesk, Inc.

Despite all the headaches, hard work, late nights, long hours, stress, pressure, personnel problems, cutthroat competition, tough decisions to make, disasters to avert, and detractors to win over, top people have very few regrets.

"Regrets? I've asked myself that many times. I don't regret anything. Life is so wonderful and I'm willing to take responsibility for everything I've done. No, I can't think of any regrets."

—**FRITZ MAYTAG**
President and brewmaster,
Anchor Brewing Company

"People like to say they have regrets because it's a lovely, romantic position to take. 'I gave up my this or that for my career,' they say. But actually they just didn't do what they didn't want to do. For their own amusement, for self-titillation, they fantasize about what they would've been doing differently or what could have happened to them. Women do it about who they married. Men do it about their job. . . . People do what they want to do and find all kinds of reasons to justify their decision."

—**RALPH ABLON**
Chairman, Ogden Corporation

"The saying that 'it's lonely at the top' is a big myth."
—**DAVID CHAMBERLAIN**
Chairman, president, and CEO, Shaklee Corporation

Success scares a lot of people. They want it until they come close to it and then they shy away. Don't let that happen to you.

The truth is that it's fun to be at the top. When you accomplish anything, no matter how small, it's fun—and chiefs accomplish a great deal. Accomplishments lead to success. Success often brings money. Money buys freedom—and fun. Finally, you get to the top by controlling your behavior, your effect on others, and other variables. That gives you a sense of being in control of your own destiny. And that feels terrific.

> "If you care for it with a passion, what you are doing becomes a labor of love. You can look up from your work at the clock and see it's nine at night and *not* say 'Oh my God, it's nine, I should have left here four hours ago.'"
>
> —TOM JORDAN
> *Owner, Jordan Vineyards*

> "On my worst days, I would not trade places with anyone on earth."
>
> —JOHN BIANCHI
> *Chairman, Bianchi International*

Do you have what it takes to make it to the top and stay there? You don't if you:

- are incompetent;
- lack emotional maturity;
- talk too much or take too much time to get to the point;
- don't understand how to make a favorable impact on people;
- are dishonest in any way, including being casual or careless with facts;
- take short cuts;
- require more supervision than is available;
- don't meet challenges head on or take advantage of opportunities;
- are an empty suit—all style and no substance;
- lack self-confidence;
- think you can rely on intelligence alone;

- don't listen;
- avoid or postpone making decisions;
- are afraid of making mistakes;
- too easily find fault in people and plans;
- have no sense of humor.

People who have those traits *and no inclination to change* do not get promoted and may even lose their jobs. However, they are the exceptions, not the rule.

I've spent my career observing and advising those on the top rungs of the corporate ladder, and I've learned that success is within everyone's reach. As I've said, top people are not magical. They simply have developed skills that the rest of us also can learn. They draw upon resources (guts, courage, luck, initiative) that also are available to you.

What qualities do top people have?

> "First and foremost, [they] have performance and competence. That comes from education, training, and exposure at the start. Then you have to be hungry, ambitious, and willing to pay the price."
>
> —GEORGE SAFIOL
> *President and COO,*
> *General Instrument Corporation*

> "Sensitivity to other people's reactions, appreciation of human values, creative imagination, reliability, physical ruggedness, financial guts, and the ability to be right 95 percent of the time."
>
> —BILL DAN
> *Chairman, Daniels Communicatu.*

> "They have no job description. The CEO's job is the only job without one to describe day-in/day-out activities other than responsibility to the outside world. At the top, you can no longer look forward to being promoted, but you can look forward to taking the helm of

the ship—motivating others to be productive, creating respect for yourself as an individual and for the company so that the institution has survivability."

—STEWART BLAIR
CEO, United Artists Entertainment Company

"They have to perform. You have to deliver the goods to stay at the top."

—GORDON PARKER
Chairman, president, and CEO,
Newmont Mining Corporation

What are top people? Top people:

- Are competent but not necessarily "off-the-charts" brilliant. They have a combination of book smarts and street smarts and the good sense to go looking for the answers they don't already have.
- Are consistent. Their moods and behavior do not swing wildly from one extreme to another.
- Fit into tomorrow's company. They learn and understand where the company is heading and support its efforts to get there.
- Are effective—able to make a positive impact on both members of their own group and other groups in the company.
- Motivate people. Through the example they set and the encouragement they give, top people help others develop and reach their potential.
- Communicate effectively up and down the ladder—not just with those with whom they are comfortable.
- Have the courage to challenge and question for the purpose of problem solving and not in a smart-alecky way.
- Have a sense of humor and use it to show humanness.
- Are creative themselves or able to recognize and appreciate others' creativity.
- Emanate relaxed rather than frenetic energy.
- Are honest.

- Fit in. Top people know and work within the corporate culture.
- Take initiative and seize opportunities. Most get promotions by making the first move to get job assignments that have visibility.
- Overcome (or at least compensate for) weaknesses and accept their own limitations without being too hard on themselves.
- Make others look good (especially their bosses). As one CEO put it, "The key to advancement is to impress the person who is your immediate boss. You move up one rung of the ladder at a time."
- Bring a solution to the table whenever they point out a problem. They don't just gripe and complain. They propose plans of action, and that really sets them apart from the rest.
- Are self-confident and comfortable with themselves as people. They have conquered their fears or learned how to cope with them and as a result can be themselves in almost any situation.

You may not fit the foregoing profile of a chief—yet. But every one of those traits is within your grasp. As you have probably realized by now, most of the recommendations I have made in this book were applications of common sense. Few are common practice, however. By practicing them in your own life on a day-in-and-day-out, minute-by-minute basis, you *will* stand out, fit in, and get ahead.

If you make a consistent effort to use the techniques I've described in this book, you can successfully control your behavior, how you affect others, and your career. As a result, you can gradually ease toward the top and take advantage of the opportunities that can ultimately bring you to your desired level of success in a chosen field. And, like the people who have made it to the top already, as long as you remain true to yourself and try to be yourself effectively at all times, you too will have few regrets.

APPENDIX

Debra Benton's Easy Reference Guide to Professional Presence

MAKE A FAVORABLE FIRST IMPRESSION

1. Use your entire physical being to express yourself. (Your physical presence is the foundation on which you build your credibility. Act in a slow, controlled, purposeful manner.)
2. Have a physical game plan. (Physically set the stage to accomplish a purpose you have decided upon ahead of time.)
3. Show people what you mean with coordinated words and actions.
4. Don't respond to distractions.
5. Develop by subtraction. (Retire your sabotaging actions— the *ineffective* things you say or do.)
6. Do the opposite of what most people do.
7. Be flexible.
8. Be willing to merely "go through the motions" for a while.
9. Remember the four-minute rule. (Be aware of and consciously control your actions for at least the first four minutes of any encounter.)

GIVE A GOOD HANDSHAKE

1. Respect people's preferences for space and distance.
2. Clasp palm to palm, not palm to fingers.
3. Talk to the person whose hand you're shaking.
4. Hold on for a split second longer than duty requires.
5. Be firm but not so forceful that you cause discomfort.
6. If you wish to convey additional warmth, use two hands.
7. Briefly and in a purposeful manner, pause again as you retrieve your hand.

REMEMBER PEOPLE'S NAMES

1. Relax; memory improves when you are at ease.
2. Immediately repeat the name aloud, using it in the very next comment you make to that person.
3. If possible and appropriate, use the name again within a few minutes.
4. At the first available opportunity, write the name down somewhere.

TOUCH IN A BUSINESS SETTING

1. Touch males and females the same way. Be consistent.
2. Be supportive, encouraging, or caring—whatever fits the situation. (Being condescending or sexually seductive is *not* the appropriate attitude for touching in any business situation.)
3. Be sensitive to the reactions of people you touch.
4. Don't sneak up from behind. Make sure that the other person is aware of your presence.
5. Plant your hand firmly on a hand, arm, or shoulder. (Touching an elbow seems most universally acceptable.)
6. Maintain physical contact for a split second.

7. Keep your hand still and steady. Do not stroke or pat.
8. Place your hand and remove it in an equally purposeful and definite manner.
9. Smile, relax, and look as if you expect the other person to accept the touch in the manner you gave it.
10. If you simply cannot bring yourself to touch physically, at least make an extra effort to convey what a touch would through your facial expression, tone of voice, and words.
11. Practice, practice, practice.

THE BUSINESS HUG

1. Expect acceptance, but if in doubt, the first time you hug, say something along the lines of "You've been so supportive, I'd like to give you a hug."
2. Grasp right hands and place your left hand around the person's shoulder, then lean your upper body toward him.
3. Turn your head so that your lips don't brush against the other person's cheek, collar, or lapel.
4. Hold the embrace a second or two longer than a typical handshake.
5. Don't touch pelvises.
6. Release the person from your embrace, look him in the eye, smile, and step back. Pause briefly and then resume your conversation, exit or do whatever else you were planning to do after the hug.

RECEIVE A BUSINESS TOUCH GRACEFULLY
(assuming it is appropriate and not an act of sexual harassment):

1. Don't act as if you've been zapped by an electric shock from a cattle prod and grimace, glare, jump, or abruptly pull back as if you're having a repulsion convulsion.
2. Allow the touch. Be aware of it. Accept it. Or merely

withstand it if you are, for some reason, repulsed or offended by it.
3. Don't read excess meaning into a touch (unless the person reaches for your wallet or worse).
4. Lean into it.
5. If possible (and comfortable for you), reciprocate.

STAND WITH PROFESSIONAL PRESENCE

1. Maintain a relaxed, energetic posture with eyes and head level.
2. Assume a neutral or "ready" position with your arms loose at your sides so they are free to gesture.
3. Stand close enough to the other person to be personal, but not so close as to be intrusive.
4. Stand upright rather than leaning against a door, wall, lectern, or furniture.
5. Don't touch yourself or: pick real or imaginary lint off your sleeves; smooth your clothing; tug at your waistband; straighten your tie; fuss with your hair; rub your hands (like Lady Macbeth attempting to scrub the "damn spot" from her hands).

SIT IN A CONTROLLED MANNER

1. Approach the chair.
2. Pause.
3. Keep your upper and lower body in alignment to stay balanced.
4. Maintaining good posture, bend your knees and purposefully lower your body.
5. Sit on the edge of the chair first.
6. Use your thigh muscles or hands to push yourself toward the back of the chair.

7. To stand up in a controlled manner, follow the same sequence in reverse.

GESTURE TO ENHANCE YOUR PRESENCE

1. Always use gestures that are appropriate for and acceptable in a specific situation. Also keep in mind that gestures which mean one thing (and have a positive impact) in the good ole USA may have a different meaning and effect in other countries.
2. When using your hands and arms, keep them away from the rib cage.
3. Hold each gesture for a split second and try to make each motion as smooth as possible.
4. Synchronize your words and actions: think of what you will say; show it; and say it. DON'T: think of what you will say; say it; and after the fact remember to show it.

USE YOUR VOICE EFFECTIVELY

1. Breathe properly.
2. Aim for variety.
3. Relax your jaw and tongue.
4. When you speak, use your entire body.
5. Start each new thought with a new breath of air and save enough breath (or take another breath) to end your thought with power.
6. Don't mistakenly conclude that the increased volume resulting from breathing properly and relaxing your jaw is too loud.
7. Don't speak hurriedly.
8. Face the person to whom you are speaking.
9. Gesture.

GET PERSONAL

1. Work on your own attitude. Become more willing to deal with others on a person-to-person basis and begin looking for common ground.
2. Reveal enough of yourself to show that you are human.
3. Ask questions; listen; give others an opportunity to talk about themselves.
4. Respect the other person's privacy with confidentiality.
5. Be consistent. Person-to-person business dealings rely on actions as well as words and are most effective when your overall management style is relatively informal.
6. Realize that abandoning role-to-role dealings and replacing them with person-to-person communication cannot be accomplished overnight. Start small and slowly.

TELL A TELLING TALE

1. Draw from your own experiences. Start a personal story collection. Describe: the situation you faced; the action you took; the result.

   Make sure your tales make a point or illustrate things you did that others may not have done.
2. Constantly add to your personal story collection. Interesting things happen to you all day long. Jot them down and use them in any situation they seem to fit.
3. Keep a file (physically or in your memory) of stories you've read or heard that made an impact on you and could have a similar effect on others.
4. When telling stories, use descriptions that incorporate as many senses as possible.
5. Be personal. Whenever possible speak to the human emotions and universal conditions that people generally have in common.
6. Vary the lengths of your anecdotes and make sure any story you tell has (and gets to) its point quickly.
7. Inject humor whenever and wherever you can.

ASK QUESTIONS EFFECTIVELY

1. Give yourself permission to ask questions. Don't wait for an invitation.
2. Ask your question in a way that truly invites a response.
3. Ask more than one question. To keep conversations flowing, query, volunteer some information of your own, then ask additional questions.
4. Use common sense and good judgment. Don't question at random or jump from topic to topic. Listen to the other person's response and tailor your next question to it.
5. Don't ask trick questions or wage probing attacks.
6. Prepare questions in advance. It's helpful to have a few preplanned questions to carry you through any conversation.
7. Listen to what is being said and what isn't. What you hear and what you don't will raise additional questions, which will, in turn, show that you were listening.
8. If you don't want to hear the answer and especially if you don't want to do anything about what you hear—don't ask the question.

BUILD SELF-CONFIDENCE

1. Relax and look back at your past successes.
2. Make sure you're in a job you enjoy and be extremely competent in that job.
3. Pat yourself on the back for every step toward a goal that you take.
4. Work on boosting others' confidence.
5. Accept and understand occasional self-doubt—but don't succumb to it.

CONTROL YOUR SELF-TALK

1. Stop putting yourself down out loud or inside your head.
2. Assign your mind a positive attitude. Mentally prepare yourself for the tasks at hand by telling yourself that you *can* do them and how you *will* accomplish them.
3. Choose the perspective you want.
4. Replace beliefs that don't work for you with ones that do. Belief determines behavior.
5. Make mental movies using affirmative self-talk as a life script. Then live it. Translate a goal into a specific, well-defined image. Then put yourself in the audience and watch your mental movie over and over again. Plant it in your subconscious. As your movie "fades out," think: "I want this to happen this way, if not better."
6. Avoid being around those who are negative.
7. Expect acceptance.
8. Remember that any disposition you do NOT manage ends up being managed by others—or running amok.

CULTIVATE AND CONVEY AN ACCEPTING ATTITUDE TOWARD OTHERS

1. If you can't be positive, be neutral. But don't be negative.
2. Consciously identify other people's positive attributes—in twenty seconds or less.
3. Don't underestimate people.
4. Don't fool yourself into thinking that you can hide your feelings from others. You can't.
5. Give compliments.
6. Realize that positive thinking and an accepting attitude toward others does not guarantee that they will behave as you wish. Don't overreact when they disappoint you.

MAKE EFFECTIVE DECISIONS

1. *Probe* for all the facts you need to make a well-informed decision. *Listen* to other people's opinions—even the ones that make it more difficult to make a decision. *Examine* all of the alternatives and consider the unconventional and unpopular ones as well as the one that seemed best to you right off the bat. *File* away the information you've gathered just in case Plan A fails and you have to switch to Plan B. *Act*—make the decision and deal with its aftermath.
2. Be willing to make the *necessary* decisions.
3. Strive for a calm attitude—not a macho or desperate surrounded-by-the-enemy stance.
4. Gather facts and opinions from as many sources as possible to get as many different points of view as possible.
5. Distill the information gathered. Consider as many alternatives as possible.
6. Listen to your intuition. If fact, intuition, or a combination of the two still do not point to a clear way to go, take a chance.
7. When you can, reduce the pressure caused by deadlines or the need to make on-the-spot decisions.
8. If time permits and it is appropriate, put the decision aside or literally sleep on it—putting it into your subconscious.
9. Make the decision.
10. If the decision is wrong, say "oops" and take corrective action.

BE COURAGEOUS

1. *Initiate. Initiate. Initiate.*
2. *Work on a particular area in which you are weak or feel uncomfortable.* At the next available opportunity to do something in that area, make at least three attempts to do it before you give up on trying.

3. *Make a list of things that are difficult or anxiety provoking for you and, on a daily basis, attempt to conquer one of the items on that personal scary-things-to-do list.* Again, don't give up until you've tried at least three times.

4. *Just forge ahead and take the appropriate risks*—no matter how nervous you feel.

5. *Have faith.* The execution may be awkward, but usually the outcome will still be good. Simply trust that axiom to prove true and jump in.

6. *Don't panic.* Most situations are not as bad as they look at first glance.

THINK!

1. Practice simple, straightforward, sequential thinking.

2. Rehash—do postmortems on past issues (looking for what went wrong *and* what went right).

3. Recognize and reward others' fresh thinking. Brainstorm.

4. Plant subjects you are considering in your subconscious.

5. Take the alternatives you have and divide them into desirable and undesirable option categories.

6. Think of what would be expected in a given situation. Then think about its opposite.

7. Put yourself in someone else's shoes.

8. Play the part of a Monday morning quarterback—only do it on Saturday. (Look at the matter as if it has already been decided and evaluate the "decision.")

9. Mentally remove constraints.

10. Create analogies.

11. Deliberately disrupt logical thought patterns.

12. Have a chat with a bartender or anyone else who is not involved or affected by the issue.

BASIC GUIDELINES FOR PUBLIC SPEAKING

1. Adjust your attitude. When speaking to fifty people, think of yourself as conducting fifty one-on-one conversations.
2. Be prepared (if possible) and talk about what you know well (if possible). Plan to: tell them what you're going to tell them; tell them; tell them what you told them.

    You can: make a point or state an opinion; then elaborate on your point using an illustration, story, or anecdote; then give the reasoning behind your point or opinion; and finally, restate your point or opinion.

    Or you can plan to: make a point or state an opinion; then elaborate on your point with an illustration, story, or anecdote; then, ask a question in order to involve the audience or your fellow panel members and get their reaction to the point(s) you made; then, recapture the audience's attention with a second story or illustration; and finally, restate your initial point or position.
3. If your schedule permits, spend time with members of the audience in advance.
4. After you have been introduced, get to the lectern in a deliberate, enthusiastic manner.
5. Stand erect with both feet firmly planted on the stage or platform.
6. Make eye contact with individual members of the audience (rather than scanning the audience with your eyes).
7. Use gestures.
8. Use humor.

ADDITIONAL PUBLIC SPEAKING TIPS

1. If you have advance notice and the time to do it, prepare a script—with pictures.
2. If possible, give your speech before you give your speech. (Try it out on colleagues, friends, dinner companions.)
3. Try not to hide behind the lectern.

4. If possible, remove your eyeglasses.

5. Beware of "reading" too much into audience members' body language.

6. If you intend using charts, overhead projections, or other audiovisual aids, rehearse with them beforehand. The proper sequence for using a flip chart is: With your hand or a pointer, draw attention to a specific point. Select one audience member to look at and talk to while making that point. *Then* speak. Repeat the same sequence for each point.

    Do *not* talk while flipping the sheet, fixing the sheet, or looking at the chart.

7. Make sure that you hold a transparency or product and receive or present a plaque "specially."

8. If you are part of a panel, remember that you are onstage all the time—and not just when you are speaking.

DURING THE QUESTION-AND-ANSWER PORTION OF YOUR PRESENTATION

1. When you are ready to take questions, let the audience know verbally AND nonverbally. Say, "Any questions?" and raise your own hand.

2. Before giving your answer, restate (and if necessary rephrase) the question.

3. After someone asks a question do not say "Good question," and do not refer to that person by name unless you are prepared to call everyone in the audience by name.

4. When answering one person's question, make eye contact with someone else.

5. Do not check with people to find out if your answer satisfied them.

6. Try to answer at least one question with a one-word response.

7. Whether you are stymied or simply want to encourage

audience participation, you always have the option of referring questions back to your audience.

WRITE SMART!

1. Know your purpose. Be succinct. Don't BS.
2. Use a simple but effective letter outline: Make the first paragraph *reader oriented*. Address the other person directly and capture his attention with a compliment or comment that "hits his hot button." Start with "you" not "I." Make the second paragraph *writer oriented*. Tell the reader why you are writing. Make the third paragraph an *action* paragraph. Inform the reader of the next action you will take.
3. Keep each paragraph short.
4. Talk to the reader in writing (with the same words you'd use while speaking).

STAY SMART—AND GET SMARTER!

1. Keep abreast of current events.
2. Keep an eye on current trends.
3. Keep up with changes in technology.
4. Be well connected personally.
5. Be sure to: think creatively; encourage creative thinking in others; look for fresh, innovative perspectives and communicate what you've learned; set aside time to develop new thought patterns and practice using them.

IF YOU HAVE THE MISFORTUNE TO BE FIRED

1. Maintain your presence. Listen carefully to exactly what is being said. If possible, write down what's being said. Don't

bother trying to get the person who is terminating you to explain or defend his position. Assume the decision that has been made is final. Don't try to change the other person's mind. It's wasted effort. Don't cry. You'll only embarrass yourself and others.

2. Ask questions. After the other person has finished talking, pause, compose yourself and then ask: *"When does this take effect?"* Find out the exact date they want you to stop working, clean out your desk, and return the office keys.

   Then ask: *"What is the financial separation package you're proposing?"* Ask about severance pay, vacation and sick pay, insurance continuance (who will be paying for it and how long will it be available), use of the office, telephone, copy machine, and so on, use of secretarial services (typing, telephone messages, etc.), and outplacement services.

3. Speak up for yourself. You have the option to ask for more. You may be surprised by what is available—if you ask. After hearing their offer, make a statement acknowledging the dismissal and asking for time to think about the separation package. When the separation package is settled, request a written agreement.

4. Hang in there. Don't tell the other person exactly what you think of him, the way he handled the dismissal, or the decision to dismiss you. Don't burn your bridges. Go home—not to a bar. Give yourself the afternoon off. Gather the family and explain the situation.

ACKNOWLEDGMENTS

With special thanks to these top people for their contributions to my book.

Norman Cousins, author
Anatomy of an Illness

Betty Lehan Harragan, author
Games Mother Never Taught You

Harvey Mackay, author
Swim with the Sharks

Don Hewitt, executive producer
"60 Minutes"

Mike Wilfley, president
A. R. Wilfley & Sons, Inc.

Peter Muller, president and
  CEO
ACA Joe Inc.

Bill Coors, chairman
Adolph Coors Company

Warren E. McCain, chairman
  and CEO
Albertson's

Fritz Maytag, president and
  brewmaster
Anchor Brewing Company

Lodwrick M. Cook, chairman
  and CEO
ARCO

Lawrence A. Weinbach,
  managing partner-CEO
Arthur Andersen & Co.

Alvar J. Green, chairman,
  president, and CEO
Autodesk, Inc.

Joseph V. Vittoria, chairman and CEO
Avis, Inc.

Timothy T. Day, president
Bar-S Foods Co.

John E. Bianchi, chairman of the board
Bianchi International

Steve Murrin, partner
Billy Bob's Texas

Carolyne Roehm, president
Carolyne Roehm, Inc.

Kal Zeff, president
CDM

Bob Greene, columnist
Chicago Tribune

Mike Hirshorn, president
Cochlear A/G Australia

Reuben Mark, chairman, president, and CEO
Colgate-Palmolive Company

Larry H. Colin, president
Colin Service Systems, Inc.

D. Dale Browning, president and CEO
Colorado National Bank of Denver

William E. Thiele, president and CEO
Continental Insurance

A. R. Carpenter, president
CSX Distribution Services

Bill Daniels, chairman
Daniels Communications

Bill Morin, chairman
Drake, Beam, Morin Inc.

Jerry Henry, senior vice-president
DuPont Electronics

Fred R. Smith, president
East/West Network

John Moore, president
Electro-Test Inc.

Joseph J. Melone, president
Equitable Life Insurance Company

William F. Farley, chairman of the board
Farley Industries/Fruit of the Loom

Bob Berkowitz, host
CNBC

John Butler, president
Financial Programs, Inc.

Jeffrey M. Cunningham, associate publisher
Forbes

Howard Solomon, president
Forest Laboratories

Marshall Loeb, managing editor
Fortune

George E. Safiol, president and COO
General Instrument Corporation

John Green, president and
CEO, Canada
Great-West Life Assurance

Russell Banks, president
Grow Group, Inc.

Harold A. Ellis, chairman of the
board and CEO
Grubb & Ellis Company

David Fanning, president
GTE Customer Network

W. Richard Kern, managing
partner
Heidrick and Struggles, Inc.

Robert L. Dilenschneider,
president and CEO
Hill and Knowlton, Inc.

William B. Wallace, president
and CEO
Home Life Insurance Company

Rose Marie Bravo, president
I. Magnin, Inc.

Yap Lim Sen, managing director
IGB Corporation Berhad

Jack Falvey, president
Intermark

John Krebbs, president
J. Parker Company

John "J" Madden, president and
CEO
John Madden Company

Glenn R. Jones, CEO
Jones Intercable, Inc.

Tom Jordan, owner
Jordan Vineyards

Tom Henrion, president
KFC National Purchasing
Cooperative, Inc.

David F. Smith, managing
director, New York
Korn/Ferry International

Sirio Maccioni, owner
Le Cirque

Jack Linkletter, president
Linkletter Enterprises

Curtis Rex Carter, Jr., chairman
Mission Bay Investments, Inc.

Robert W. Galvin, chairman of
the Executive Committee
Motorola, Inc.

Tom Freston, president and
CEO
MTV Networks

R. Michael Franz, president
and CEO
Murata Business Systems, Inc.

John A. Ziegler, Jr., president
National Hockey League

Bob Graves, founder
National Marrow Donor
Program

Neil Georgi, president
Georgi & Associates, Inc.

Richard Torrenzano, senior
vice-president
New York Stock Exchange

Gordon R. Parker, chairman, president, and CEO
Newmont Mining Corporation

Dr. Armand Hammer, chairman and CEO
Occidental Petroleum

Ralph E. Ablon, chairman of the board
Ogden Corporation

Michael S. Lesser, president
Ogilvy & Mather

Thomas G. Plaskett, chairman, president, and CEO
Pan-American Corporation

Bob Hunter, president
PepsiCo Food Systems

Einar Kloster, president and CEO
Philips Lighting Holding B.V.

John M. Richards, president and COO
Potlatch Corporation

Roger Werner, president and CEO
Primesports Ventures

Dave Liniger, CEO
RE/MAX International

Alex J. Mandl, chairman and CEO
Sea Land Service, Inc.

Jeff Smulyan, owner
Seattle Mariners

David M. Chamberlain, chairman, president, and CEO
Shaklee Corporation

Thomas J. Neff, president
Spencer Stuart

Ernie Howell, retired president
St. Regis/WPM

Louis P. Mattis, chairman and CEO
Sterling Drug Inc.

Ryal Poppa, chairman, president, and CEO
Storage Technology Corporation

Richard Storck, president
Storck Development

Phil Wilkinson, director network systems
Strategic Business Planning AT&T

Ronald Unkefer, chairman and CEO
The Good Guys

Andrew Sherwood, senior partner
The Goodrich & Sherwood Company

Robert H. B. Baldwin, chairman
The Lodestar Group

W. Ted Wright IV, managing director
The Regent of Sydney

Alfred T. McNeill, chairman, president, and CEO
The Turner Corporation

Robert L. Bartley, editor
The Wall Street Journal

J. Richard Munro, chairman of
the executive committee
Time Warner Inc., ATC
Corporation

Tatsuro Toyoda, executive vice-
president, member of the
board
Toyota Motor Corporation

Dave Carpenter, chairman,
president, and CEO
Transamerica Occidental Life
Insurance

Robin Mangos, managing
director
Travelseekers International

Dave Powelson, president
TRI-R Systems

Stewart Blair, CEO
United Artists Entertainment
Company

Elmo R. Zumwalt, Jr., retired,
admiral, chief of operations
United States Navy

Gary Hart, former senator
United States Senate

John H. Callen, Jr., chairman
and CEO
Ward Howell International

Winthrop Rockefeller,
chairman, CEO
Winrock Farms, Inc.

Thomas J. Bickett, president
and CEO
Witco Corporation

David K. Lam, managing
director
Yuen Loong Group of
Companies

Jim Rupp, Attorney